James Ker-Lindsay

Britain and the Cyprus Crisis

1963 - 1964

PELEUS

STUDIEN ZUR ARCHÄOLOGIE UND
GESCHICHTE GRIECHENLANDS UND ZYPERNS

BAND 27

James Ker-Lindsay

Britain and the Cyprus Crisis

1963 - 1964

BIBLIOPOLIS
Mannheim und Möhnesee 2004

PELEUS
Studien zur Archäologie und Geschichte Griechenlands und Zyperns
Herausgegeben von Reinhard Stupperich und Heinz A. Richter
Band 27

Cover vignettes:
Front Cover: Archbishop Makarios and Vice-President Kuchuk on a visit to the Sovereign Base Areas after Cypriot independence. (courtesy PIO, Nicosia).
Opposite title page: Cup by the Peithinos painter, Berlin, Pergamonmuseum (CVA Berlin 2, Taf. 61).

Gesamtherstellung: Druck Partner Rübelmann GmbH, Carl-Benz-Str. 11, 69 502 Hemsbach

BIBLIOPOLIS
D - 59519 Möhnesee-Wamel, Schulpatt 13
Tel. 02924/2781, Fax 02924/2757, e-mail: bibliopolis@web.de

ISBN 3-933925-58-4

Contents

For My Family and Biljana

Acknowledgements

Many of the insights in this volume came from interviews with people closely involved with the events of 1963-64. In particular, I would like to thank the following: Dr Thomas Adams, Rauf Denktash, Chris Economides, Necati Munir Ertekun, Ahmet Gazioglu, Vassos Lyssarides, Zaim Necatigil, Ozdemir Ozgur, Tassos Papadopoulos and Christodoulos Veniamin. Similarly, I would like to acknowledge the help I received from Spyros Kyprianou, Osman Orek and Andreas Ziartides. There were also a number of other individuals, both Greek and Turkish Cypriot, who did not wish to be quoted directly. Their contribution was also vital. My gratitude also goes to the staff at the Public Records Office in Kew and at the Press and Information Office in Nicosia for all their valuable assistance.

I would next like to say thank you to all those who provided guidance and help during the writing and editing of this work: Professor AJR Groom, Professor Andrew Williams and Dr Jarrod Wiener at the University of Kent and Dr Michael Pugh at Plymouth University. I would also like to say an extra special thank you to Professor Keith Webb, who ended up having a far closer involvement with this work than he ever expected. Most recently, I would like to express my appreciation to Professor Heinz Richter for graciously accepting this work for publication as part of the *Peleus* series.

Finally, I would like to thank the friends and colleagues who helped me during the extensive period spent preparing this volume. I would especially like to say thank you to my good friends Dr Oliver Richmond and Matthew Watkins. They both provided much needed laughs along the way. However, a special debt of gratitude is owed to my family – my parents, my grandmother, Mark, John, Adam, Laura and my wife, Biljana – for all the support they have provided over the years.

Introduction

The breakdown of peace in Cyprus cannot be an isolated event. Turkey and Greece are inevitably involved, and with them the whole delicate strategic balance of the eastern Mediterranean and the southeast flank of NATO. Cyprus is wired like a detonator to other larger problems.[1]

Although a relatively small island, Cyprus has had a rich and diverse history. Just 3,572 square miles in size it sits at the historical crossroads between the East and West. Turkey, its nearest neighbour, lies just forty miles from its northern coast. To the east, Syria is only seventy-five miles away. Rhodes, the nearest large Greek island, and Egypt are roughly two hundred and fifty miles west and south respectively. Mainland Greece lies approximately five hundred miles west. As a result, the island has been regarded as vital territory by almost every empire that has wished to assert control over the wider Eastern Mediterranean region. Over the course of the past four thousand years Cyprus has been conquered, ruled or colonised by an impressive array of civilisations: Minoans, Assyrians, Persians, Romans, Byzantines, Arabs, Franks, Genoese, Venetians, Ottomans and, most recently, the British.

After a long history of being controlled by others, Cyprus finally became independent in August 1960. However, and perhaps uniquely in the modern era, that independence was curtailed by a series of agreements signed with and between outside parties. The complex constitutional arrangements put in place entrusted the ultimate protection of the new country's constitution, sovereignty, independence and territorial integrity to Greece, Turkey and Britain. Under the terms of the Treaty of Guarantee, these three countries, the 'Guarantor Powers', were given an exclusive right, collectively or independently, to intervene if events on the island so required. As Article IV of the Treaty states,

> *In the event of a breach of the provisions of the present Treaty, Greece, Turkey and the United Kingdom undertake to consult together with respect to the representations or measures necessary to ensure observance of those provisions.*
>
> *In so far as common or concerted action may not prove possible, each of the three guaranteeing powers reserves the right to take action with the sole aim of re-establishing the state of affairs created by the present Treaty.*

1 Urquhart, *A Life in Peace and War*, p.199

Although the Treaty clearly states that consultation is expected prior to any action by the Guarantor Powers, it is not difficult to see that this arrangement posed serious problems and dangers. Could Greece and Turkey really reach an agreement in the event that developments on the island threatened to destabilise the constitutional arrangements that had been put in place? Perhaps the more important question was whether Greece and Turkey would be ready and able to lean on their respective communities sufficiently to ensure that a problem was not created in the first place?

With the benefit of hindsight, this second question was indeed the more important of the two. While independence had certainly been welcomed as a means of preventing a prolongation of the direct bilateral Greek-Turkish stand-off that had developed over Cyprus in the second half of the 1950s, independence had instead created a new, potentially more dangerous, security problem insofar as the Cypriot communities were now expected to overlook the differences that had arisen over the course of the EOKA campaign and work together to build a state based on equality and mutual respect. With little experience of self-government and the monumental task of creating a nation from a state that commanded little respect from either community, the danger of conflict on the island was a constant threat. This threat was further amplified by the presence of Greek and Turkish troops on the island as a part of the Treaty of Alliance. These forces made it more likely that if fighting broke out Greece and Turkey would be dragged into direct confrontation. If fighting were to take place on the island it would not be difficult to envisage the conditions that could see hostilities rapidly extend beyond the shores of the island and lead to direct confrontation between the two countries in the Aegean Sea or on their shared land border in Thrace.

Although the prospect of a war between Greece and Turkey was serious in its own right, it became all the more worrying in view of the fact that both countries were members of NATO. Turkey, in particular, was regarded as a vital component of the NATO's security against the Soviet Union as it was West's only direct non-arctic route into the USSR. Obviously any strains between Greece and Turkey would limit Turkey's effectiveness as a frontline state. Moreover, a Greek-Turkish war was widely seen as offering just the type of distraction Moscow could use to good effect, either in the region or on the wider international stage. Just as the 1956 Suez Crisis had provided good cover for the Soviet suppression of a rebellion in Hungary, another conflict in Eastern Mediterranean could also be exploited. In this light, the small island of Cyprus truly was, as Sir Brian Urquhart noted, 'wired like a detonator to other larger problems'. For better or for worse, Britain had been given an explicit role to ensure that Cyprus did not ignite a larger problem.

It is within this wider context that Britain's role under the 1960 constitution should be seen and analysed. As the nominally impartial signatory of the Treaty of Guarantee, the United Kingdom was always expected to play the part of the neutral referee. Under normal conditions, Britain would be expected to be a source of balance, regulating the affairs of the island at the regular meetings held between the Guarantor Powers. However, in the event that any disturbance took place on the island that could threaten to lead to a confrontation between Greece and Turkey, it would be up to the United Kingdom to play the part of peacemaker. While this fact was well, if only tacitly, understood at the time of Cypriot independence, few in Britain expected that this role would be put to the test just three short years after the Union flag was lowered over the island in August 1960. However, in December 1963, just forty months after Cyprus became independent, an outbreak of fighting drew the United Kingdom back into the island's politics.

Britain and the Cyprus Crisis, 1963-64

This work is an attempt to cast light on the actions of the United Kingdom during the Cyprus Crisis of 1963-64. The work concentrates on a very specific period of events, charting the course of British actions from the start of fighting to the moment when UN Security Council Resolution 186 passed responsibility for peacekeeping and peacemaking over to the United Nations. In essence, Britain actually undertook several different, but interconnected roles during this period. On the one hand, Britain had a part to play as a crisis manager and peacekeeper. Its timely decision, along with Greece and Turkey, to establish a peacekeeping force, the Joint Truce Force, certainly helped to limit the extent of fighting on the island, and thus reduced the chance of direct Turkish intervention. However, as this work shows, it was not an easy role to play. Secondly, Britain tried to act as peacemaker. At first this was done informally on the island, but was later supplemented by a formal peace process in London. Unfortunately, the process failed in its objective and in doing so created a rift between Britain and the Greek Cypriots, which ended all hopes that Britain might be able to broker a compromise between the parties. It also affected Britain's efforts to find an alternative peacekeeping force to replace the Joint Truce Force.

The need for a replacement for the Joint Truce Force became very clear with the failure of the London Conference. Initial British attention focused on NATO and its potential pacification role on the island, either as a distinct organisation or indirectly through an operation staged by a number of its member states. This was eventually rejected by the Greek Cypriots. The Commonwealth was then considered as a possible option, but found little support in London. In the end, and following considerable debate, the UN took charge for maintaining peace and stability on the island. This was in many ways a controversial decision as the idea of UN peacekeeping had been strongly rejected by Britain at the start of the crisis. Indeed, even into February the idea of UN peacekeeping was resisted in London. Therefore, this work will examine the transformation of Britain's attitudes about UN involvement, from initial opposition to any form of United Nations involvement through to the decision to take the matter before the UN Security Council and its subsequent acceptance of UN Resolution 186.

Wider issues and questions

Quite apart from the way in which Britain led attempts to try to prevent a wider war between Greece and Turkey from erupting, the period from December 1963-March 1964 is particularly notable for two other reasons, both of which were to prove profoundly important for the future of the island.

First of all, it was during these months that the Greek Cypriots were accorded international legitimacy as the Government of the Republic of Cyprus. As will be shown, this recognition came about partly as a requirement of international peacekeeping and peacemaking efforts. However, it also becomes clear that the actual confirmation of this recognition involved a certain amount of what the Turkish Cypriots see as betrayal – betrayal by Britain, by the United States, and, most surprisingly, by Turkey. This development was a major victory for the Greek Cypriots.

On the other hand, and secondly, this period saw the acceptance by the international community of the legality of the Treaty of Guarantee. During the period analysed in this work, the Greek Cypriots unsuccessfully tried to abrogate the Treaty. The result of this failure was not only that Turkey retained a constitutional right to intervene, but that this was clearly accepted by the international community. This right was put into effect in 1974 after a coup ordered by the then military government in Athens overthrew Archbishop Makarios, the first president of the independent state. As a result the island was divided and the more modern understanding of the 'Cyprus Problem' was created. Ankara's right to take such a step was effectively recognised during the period discussed in this book.

Earlier research on the 1963-64 Cyprus Crisis

Despite of the clear importance of the period, not just in terms of being the first major outbreak of inter-communal fighting on the island but also insofar as it set the parameters for certain key aspects of the Cyprus issue, there has, until relatively recently, very little by way of systematic and in-depth research has so far been conducted. With the notable exception of Alan James's work on the peacekeeping aspects of the 1963-64 Cyprus Crisis,[2] published in 2002, there has been little distinct academic attention paid to this era of Cypriot history. Instead the period has usually tended to be treated as a transitional phase within the large number of works that have been written on the domestic history of Cyprus or on the origins and evolution of the Cyprus Problem in a wider context. Even the works looking at the post-Resolution 186 operations of the United Nations in Cyprus devote little more than a few words to the period.[3] Fortunately, there have been a number of accounts

---

2 Alan James, *Keeping the Peace in the Cyprus Crisis, 1963-64.*

3 For example: Karl Birgisson, 'United Nations Peacekeeping Force in Cyprus', pp.221-223. United Nations Department of Public Information *The Blue Helmets*, pp.283-286. Fabian, *Soldiers Without Enemies*, p.265. Harbottle, *The Impartial Soldier*, pp.7-18. James, *Peacekeeping in International Politics*, pp.224-226. Luard, *A History of the United Nations, Volume 2,* pp.407-413. Papadopoulos, *Peace-Making and Peacekeeping by the United Nations. Cyprus. A Case Study*, pp.22-23. Parsons, *From Cold War to Hot Peace*, pp.172-173. Rikhye et al. *The Thin Blue Line*, pp.99-100. Urquhart, *Ralph Bunche,* pp.368-369. Verrier, *International Peacekeeping*, pp.81-83. Wainhouse, *International Peace Observation*, pp. 437-446. White, *Keeping the Peace*, p.241.

written by those directly involved with the events of that time.[4] However, as is usually the case, while these narratives add a great deal to the overall picture of that time, they are in many cases incomplete reference sources. Some deliberately present the situation from one particular standpoint. In other cases no attempt is made to construct a wider picture.

It would be wrong, however, to suggest that the period has been left wholly unexamined. Apart from the James book, there have been some other excellent accounts of those months.[5] However, these still do not provide the thorough account that the period deserves or needs. It is with this in mind that this work attempts to try to redress this situation, even if only partially, by providing some insights into the British response to events taking place at that time. Importantly, the analysis is not solely confined to Britain's efforts to engage in crisis management and peacemaking through diplomacy, both on the island and at the international level. The work also examines Britain's vital and commendable peacekeeping efforts from the start of the crisis, on 23 December 1963, until the very moment responsibility for keeping the peace was handed over to the United Nations, with the passing on UN Security Council Resolution 186 on 4 March 1964.

The structure of the work

The book is structured around three distinct phases of the crisis. Following an introduction to the history of Anglo-Cypriot relations and the process of constitutional collapse, contained in Chapter 1, the second and third chapters examine the initial reactions to the outbreak of violence on the island. Chapter 2 explains how fighting erupted in Nicosia on 23 December and how this quickly proliferated to other towns. The concern of the Guarantor Powers led to the creation of the Joint Truce Force, which, although nominally tripartite in nature, was in reality a solely British undertaking. Chapter 3 looks at how the Truce Force consolidated its position and examines the first attempt at peacemaking. In particular, the section covers the visit of Duncan Sandys, the British Commonwealth Secretary, and his efforts to convene a peace conference in London in mid-January.

The second phase of the crisis is covered in chapters four, five and six. Chapter 4 examines the London Conference and explains how and why the peacemaking effort failed. It will also show how events at that time directly helped the Greek Cypriots to be recognised as having lawful control over the Cyprus Government and how the failure of the London Conference led to a growth in anti-British sentiment amongst Greek Cypriots, which in turn led Britain to approach the United States for assistance in putting together a peacekeeping force based on NATO. The chapter also looks at the evolution of ideas about peacekeeping based on NATO or the Commonwealth. Chapter 5 traces the efforts to put

---

4 Ball, *The Past Has Another Pattern*, pp.337-346. Bitsios, *Cyprus. The Vulnerable Republic*, pp.126-157. Clerides, *Cyprus. My Deposition*, (Volumes 1 & 2, *passim*). Urquhart, *A Life in Peace and War*, pp.197-198.

5 In particular: Joseph, *Cyprus. Ethnic Conflict and International Concern*. Nicolet, *United States Policy Towards Cyprus, 1954-1974*, pp.188-224. Smith, "At Arm's Length: NATO and the United Nations in the Cold War Era", pp.68-71. Sonyel, *Cyprus: the Destruction of a Republic*. Verrier, "Cyprus: Britain's Security Role". Windsor, *NATO and the Cyprus Crisis*.

together a NATO peacekeeping force and shows how this failed as a direct result of the resistance put up by Archbishop Makarios. Chapter 6 starts with an account of how the Soviet Union became involved in efforts to prevent the reformulation of previous ideas for the creation of a NATO-based peacekeeping force and how this eventually led Britain to pass responsibility for handling the search for a peacekeeping force to the United States. The chapter concludes with Britain's letter to the President of the UN Security Council asking for an urgent meeting to discuss the Cyprus issue.

The last two chapters cover the final phase of the crisis, when the issue of Cyprus was discussed at the United Nations. Chapter 7 examines how the various parties prepared for the debate and charts the course of the first crucial days of discussion on the floor of the Security Council and how the efforts of the Secretary-General to reach a compromise on a resolution failed, only to be taken up by five of the non-permanent members of the Council. The final chapter, Chapter 8, covers the final days of the debate and the eventual vote to pass UN Security Council Resolution 186, on 4 March 1964, which finally extricated Britain from its role as peacekeeper and crisis manager.

After summarising the events, the Conclusion evaluates Britain's actions over the course of the crisis and identifies the main reasons why the United Kingdom became involved. Additionally, the chapter also looks at the crisis in wider international terms. An analysis of the actions of Greece and Turkey, the other two Guarantor Powers, is also provided, as is an assessment of the parts played by the United States and the Soviet Union. A further section is devoted to an analysis of why the Non-Aligned Movement ended playing almost no role in the crisis, even though Cyprus was a member. Finally, the chapter ends with an analysis of the Joint Truce Force and explains why the Force could never have successfully overseen a long term conflict management role on the island, despite the fact that it was clearly a peacekeeping operation in both name and nature.

1

The Origins of the Crisis

Unlike other colonial possessions, Cyprus was never intended to be a source of wealth or prestige. From the moment Britain took control of the administration of Cyprus from the Ottoman Empire, in 1878, the sole purpose of the island was to provide protection for the Suez Canal and thereby help to ensure a clear passage to India, the most important British colonial possession. In return for gaining these administrative rights over the island, London gave the Ottoman Empire an undertaking that it would help repel any Russian attack on its eastern provinces. Similarly, the agreement reached between the two empires also stipulated that if Moscow returned the territories captured during the 1877-78 Russo-Turkish War, Britain would hand the island back to full Ottoman rule.

Despite the apparently temporary nature of the arrangement between London and Constantinople, the transfer was nonetheless welcomed by the island's majority Greek population. They expected Britain to be sympathetic to their aspiration for *Enosis* – the union of the island with the Kingdom of Greece. This hope was no doubt fuelled by the key role played by Britain in securing Greek Independence in the 1820s. Their belief that this might actually happen was further encouraged by the statements made in support of this by prominent philhellenes, such as William Gladstone, the leader of the Liberal Party.[1] Indeed, it was with this in mind that the first High Commissioner of the island, Sir Garnet Wolsely, was greeted on his arrival by a group of leading Greek Cypriot dignitaries, including the Bishop of Kitium, appealing for the island to be ceded to Greece.[2] They were to be bitterly disappointed. Unlike Gladstone, Prime Minister Disraeli had little sympathy for the Greek cause and certainly had no intention of giving up such a valuable piece of territory and by the time Gladstone took office in 1880 it seemed decided that Cyprus would remain firmly under British control – despite the fact that it could not provide a deep water harbour and was therefore of little naval value. Even the establishment of a formal British garrison in Egypt, in 1882, did nothing to diminish London's wish to retain authority over Cyprus.

In 1914 the island was formally annexed by Britain following the decision of the Ottoman Empire to side with Germany at the start of the First World War. The following year London came very close to giving the Greek Cypriots what they hoped for when Cyprus was offered to Greece as an inducement to the Greeks to meet their treaty obligations to Serbia and join the war. Even though the plan was supported by Eleftherios Venizelos, the Prime Minister, the offer was rejected by the Greek King, Constantine I.

---

1 Richmond, *Mediating in Cyprus. The Cypriot Communities and the United Nations*, p.69
2 Sonyel, *Cyprus: the Destruction of a Republic. British Documents, 1960-65*, p.3

British control over Cyprus was further strengthened in 1923 when, under the terms of the Treaty of Lausanne, the newly formed Turkish Republic formally relinquished its claims to Cyprus. This decision was made in spite of the fact that the eastern provinces cited in the 1878 Treaty had been returned to Turkey by the new Soviet Government in 1918. Moreover, Kemal Ataturk, the founding President of the new Turkish Republic, called upon Turkish Cypriots to leave the island and settle in Turkey. This idea was rejected by most Turkish Cypriots, who were appalled at the living conditions in Anatolia at the time.[3] On 10 March 1925 Britain formally declared Cyprus a Crown Colony.

The removal of these last vestiges of formal Turkish sovereignty over the island quickly led to renewed calls for *Enosis* from the Greek Cypriots These were consistently rejected. In 1931 Greek Cypriot frustrations reached boiling point and violent riots broke out. In response, the colonial authority adopted a number of measures to prevent similar incidents in future, including banning the flying of the Greek flag, prohibiting political parties, and increasing press censorship. Needless to say, these steps did little to dampen pro-union sentiment and following a break in nationalist activity during the Second World War, when the Greek Cypriots expressed loyalty to the British Empire, by the end of the 1940s frustration had once again surfaced within the Greek Cypriot community about continued British rule over the island.

The path to independence

On 15 January 1950 the Ethnarchy Council, the Church-led supreme leadership of the Greek Cypriot community, held an island-wide plebiscite on the question of *Enosis*. The vote revealed that 96% of participating Greek Cypriots wished to see the island's union with Greece. In response the Turkish Cypriots, with the support of the United Kingdom, presented a document to the United Nations in which they outlined their opposition to any moves to cede the island to Greece.[4] However, the cause was now firmly established and received another major boost soon afterwards when the young, politically motivated Bishop of Kition, thirty-seven year old Michael Mouskos, was elected Archbishop and took the title Makarios III.

At the same time the Greek Cypriots were becoming more active in their agitation for *Enosis*, the Greek Government started to take a more active interest in the future of the island. This marked a departure from previous practice. Earlier Greek Governments had avoided taking a position on Cyprus for fear of alienating Britain, which provided Greece with economic aid and political support. However, in 1953 the Greek Prime Minister, Field Marshal Alexandros Papagos, met with the British Foreign Secretary, Sir Anthony Eden, and broached the subject of Cyprus. Eden refused to discuss the issue. Outraged at the rude way in which he had been treated, Papagos adopted a far more forthright stand on the Cyprus question. As a result, on 3 May 1954, the Greek Prime Minister made a public

---

3 Crawshaw, *The Cyprus Revolt. An Account of the Struggle for Union with Greece*, p.2

4 Michaelides, "The Turkish Cypriot Working Class and the Cyprus Labour Movement", p.47

commitment to take the matter to the United Nations. The United Kingdom responded that the matter was an internal issue and therefore it was not subject to consideration by the organisation. A resolution put forward by New Zealand, on 17 December 1954, postponed any discussion of the Cyprus issue. [5]

Discussions now turned to other ways in which to achieve *Enosis*, including by force of arms.[6] In early 1951 Makarios had met George Grivas, a retired colonel of the Greek Army who had been born in Cyprus, and as the route for political solution appeared to have been blocked Grivas was permitted to step up his plans for a military campaign to end British rule and unite Cyprus with Greece. Despite the rumours of a build up of weapons, the British authorities appeared to underestimate the danger of an armed struggle and it was not until January 1955, when a small Greek fishing boat was stopped and boarded by the British Navy and found to be carrying a considerable quantity of weapons, that the true level of the threat became apparent. However, it was too late to stop halt the preparations for a rebellion and, on 1 April 1955 a series of bombs exploded at key administrative buildings around the island. The EOKA uprising had begun.[7]

Despite its stated intention of achieving *Enosis*, EOKA (National Organisation of Cypriot Fighters) at first attempted to take a conciliatory line with the island's minority Turkish Cypriot community. In July of that year it issued a pamphlet, in Turkish, explaining its position and clarifying that the struggle was aimed at the British and not the Turkish Cypriots.[8] Nonetheless, the Turkish Cypriot community rejected any association with EOKA, preferring to remain under British rule rather than live under Greek administration. In fact, the community actively sided with the colonial authorities and many joined the Cypriot police, thereby making up for the absence of a large number of Greek Cypriots that had left the ranks following the start of the EOKA campaign. Furthermore elements of the Turkish Cypriot community formed a counter movement to *Enosis*. Called Volkan (Volcano), the new organisation employed similar guerrilla tactics to EOKA. The organisation was later re-structured with support from Turkey and changed its name to the Turkish Resistance Movement (TMT).[9]

By the summer of 1955, events had taken a turn for the worse and violence engulfed the island. In August, the United Kingdom called a conference to discuss issues of eastern Mediterranean peace and security, namely the Cyprus issue. This event marked a monumental turning point in the affairs of the island as the British Government invited Greece and Turkey to attend. By doing so the United Kingdom was announcing that the matter was not an internal matter but directly involved the two 'motherlands'. As Eden explained in his memoirs, which were written before Cypriot independence,

---

5 For an account of the UN debates in the 1950s see Xydis, *Cyprus. Conflict and Reconciliation 1954-1958*. See also Faustmann, "The Historical Background to the UN's Involvement in Cyprus", Richmond and Ker-Lindsay (eds.), *The Work of the UN in Cyprus. Promoting Peace and Development*, pp.3-49

6 Clerides, *Cyprus. My Deposition* (Volume 1), p.30

7 For a comprehensive account of this period see Holland, *Britain and the Revolt in Cyprus, 1954-59.*

8 Salih, *Cyprus. The Impact of Diverse Nationalism on a State*, p.9

9 *House of Commons Foreign Affairs Select Committee on Cyprus, 3rd Report*, p.1

> In geography and in tactical considerations, the Turks have the stronger claim in Cyprus; in race and language, the Greeks; in strategy, the British, so long as their industrial life depends on oil supplies from the Persian Gulf. Progress in self-government could not be made until these claims were reconciled, and one of two methods had to be chosen. Greeks and Turks could be associated with the British in control of the island, or the island could be partitioned.[10]

Of course this was a double-edged sword. To the Greek Cypriots the invitation extended to Greece appeared to be an acknowledgement that their position as a part of the wider Hellenic world was accepted by Britain. However, Makarios was furious about the invitation to Turkey, accusing the British Government of re-igniting a Turkish interest in Cyprus that had been doused by Ankara thirty years earlier. The Archbishop therefore refused to attend. The talks went ahead anyway but were to be clouded by more violence. In retaliation to perceived Greek Cypriot political extremism in Cyprus, anti-Greek riots broke out in the Turkish cities of Istanbul and Izmir. The conference soon broke down.

Britain now decided to take a tougher approach to security in Cyprus. The civilian Governor of the island was recalled and in his place London installed the former Chief of the Imperial Staff, Field Marshal Sir John Harding. True to military form, Harding soon set to work radically altering the United Kingdom's approach to the problem. In addition to increasing the number of troops in the island, harsh new measures were introduced that included the imposition of the death penalty for a range of offences and the internment of suspected EOKA members. However, Harding was also aware of the need to reach a political solution and soon entered into negotiations with the Archbishop.[11] Despite agreeing to meet with Harding, Makarios nonetheless remained firm in his demand that the Greek Cypriots be granted the right of self-determination, and therefore *Enosis*, even though he knew full well that Britain's view of Turkey's overriding strategic importance necessarily ruled out such a solution.[12] Still, Makarios remained committed to the demand and believed that Greece, the United States and the United Nations were unwilling blindly to accept Britain's argument concerning the importance of Turkey.[13] After five months of negotiation with the Archbishop, no drop in the level of violence, and no evidence that he was prepared to call for a cessation of hostilities over which he was regarded as having a considerable say, the decision was taken by the British Government, in early-March 1956, to deport the Archbishop to the Seychelles. The hope was that this would deprive EOKA of its momentum. It this regard the move was successful. However, the other intention of the

---

10 Eden, *Full Circle*, p.415

11 Holland described the discussions as having been, 'one of the most protracted and complex exchanges in the history of British decolonization after the Second World War' Holland, *op. cit.*, p85. See also Markides, "Britain's 'New Look' Policy for Cyprus and Makarios-Harding Talks, January 1955-March 1956".

12 Eden, *op. cit.*, p.405

13 *Ibid.*, p.405

move had been to try to encourage a new, more moderate leadership of the Greek Cypriot community that might be amenable to British thinking. This failed.[14]

In the meantime the British Government enlisted the aid of the eminent jurist Lord Radcliffe in an attempt to draft a new plan for self-government. With this new phase in progress, Harding went on an all-out offensive against EOKA. Troop numbers were increased and by the autumn of 1956 the island was buzzing as thirty thousand British soldiers attempted to defeat Colonel Grivas and his forces. Controversially, Harding also started to authorise the execution of convicted EOKA members.

Meanwhile, the island appeared to take on a new strategic importance. In 1954, the British Garrison in Egypt had been forced to leave when the new government led by Colonel Nasser refused to renew the treaty allowing them to guard the Suez Canal. Following this, the headquarters of Britain's military presence in the region had shifted to Cyprus. Moreover, air power gave the island an important role as an 'unsinkable aircraft carrier'. The value of Cyprus was highlighted in November 1956 when, following Nasser's decision to nationalise the Suez Canal, Britain and France used Cyprus as the main base for the invasion of Egypt.[15] In the aftermath of the Suez Crisis the first signs appeared that London was changing its views on the Cyprus issue. Importantly, Turkey appeared to be given more weight as Britain realised that its dominance over the region was waning.

However, the prospects for a negotiated settlement to the uprising were to remain as distant as ever. In December 1956, Lord Radcliffe presented his ideas. They were immediately rejected by the Greek Government. Shortly afterwards, in early 1957, Prime Minister Eden resigned and was replaced by the Foreign Secretary, Harold Macmillan. This heralded a new phase in the negotiation process. Britain now accepted the possibility of partition, *Taksim* – an idea that was being promoted by the Turkish Cypriot community in response to call for *Enosis*.[16] Furthermore, Macmillan quickly made clear his personal commitment to reaching a negotiated solution, rather than continue with the heavy-handed military approach to restoring calm. With no leader to replace Makarios emerging from the Greek Cypriot Community, the decision was therefore taken, in March 1957, to free the Archbishop from his exile. Rather than return to Cyprus, however, Makarios chose to settle in Greece. As a result, there was no further improvement of the situation in Cyprus and little hope for a solution. Therefore, when Harding's two year tenure of the post of Governor of Cyprus came to an end, it was announced that there would be a return to a civilian governor. On 3 December 1957, Sir Hugh Foot took over.

Foot took a new approach to internal security. He downplayed the military attempts to beat EOKA and emphasized his desire for constructive and open dialogue. At the same time the idea of self-government leading to self-determination was formulated. This time the

14 Hatzivassiliou, "Blocking Enosis: Britain and the Cyprus Question, March-December 1956", p.248

15 It is interesting to note that with the increased British military presence on the island in advance of the attack, EOKA actually stepped up its campaign. During November 416 attacks killed over forty people, many of whom were service personnel. Vanezis, *Makarios. Life and Leadership*, p.124

16 Hatzivassiliou, *op. cit.*, p.261

proposal was rejected by the Turkish Cypriots, on the advice of Ankara, on the grounds that they felt that it would inevitably lead to *Enosis*.[17] A few months later, in June 1958, another proposal was put forward, the Macmillan Plan, which called for the United Kingdom, Greece and Turkey to take joint responsibility for the administration of the island for seven years, after which a decision would be taken on the future of Cyprus. The plan was immediately rejected by Greece and the Greek Cypriots, who saw the plan as a first step towards partition of the island.

By this time the internal situation had deteriorated significantly. The EOKA campaign was now in its fourth year and the Turkish Cypriots had in that time mustered a considerable number of men and arms within their own militia, TMT. As the prospect of civil war looked increasingly likely, the British colonial authorities launched a crackdown on both EOKA and TMT.[18] With tensions now dangerously high between the two communities on the island, Makarios made a monumental move. In September 1958 he announced that independence, rather than *Enosis*, would be acceptable for Cyprus. This decision came at the same time as London appeared ready to give in and had announced that it would be prepared to see Greece and Turkey settle the matter of Cyprus bilaterally.

In January 1959, representatives of the Greek and Turkish Governments met in the Swiss city of Zurich. By 11 February the two governments had agreed that Cyprus would become independent. A week later a conference was convened in London attended by Greece, Turkey, the United Kingdom, and both the Greek and Turkish Cypriot communities. All the delegates ratified the agreement even though Makarios had been concerned about the implications of the new structure regarding the desire of the Greeks Cypriots for eventual union with Greece.

In the months that followed the exact terms of Britain's post independence position on the island were debated. While London wanted to retain a fairly substantial area of the island for its own use, Makarios was determined to ensure that Britain's bases would be as small as possible. After several months of haggling it was finally agreed that Britain would retain two bases as sovereign territory, which altogether amounted to ninety-nine square miles. The larger of the two would be Episkopi to the west of the island, near Limassol, which also incorporated an airfield at Akrotiri. The second, smaller base was Dhekelia, which was located near Larnaca and would also incorporate the important intelligence facilities at Ayios Nikolaos. Additionally, the United Kingdom would retain special rights of access to a number of other areas that were deemed to be of importance. However, these areas would officially be the territory of the Republic of Cyprus. The most notable site in this category was RAF Nicosia.

Despite having accepted the terms of the Zurich-London Agreements, including the package that gave Britain continued sovereignty over three per cent of the island, all of which was clearly in contrast to the Greek Cypriots' hope for *Enosis*, Makarios was nevertheless elected president of the new republic by the Greek Cypriots. As per the new

---

17 Salih, *op. cit.*, p.12

18 Panteli, *A New History of Cyprus*, p.180

constitution, the Turkish Cypriots elected Dr Fazil Kuchuk, a prominent publisher who had led the Turkish Cypriot delegation in London, as the new state's vice-president. On the 16 August 1960, Britain departed and the Republic of Cyprus came into being.

Independence and constitutional breakdown

Within a year Cyprus had become a member of the United Nations, the Council of Europe, and the Commonwealth of Nations. Significantly, Cyprus also became a member of the Non-Aligned Movement. This decision was taken despite opposition from the Turkish Cypriot leadership. However, the constitutional veto that was given to the vice-president was not used by Kuchuk who accepted Turkey's argument that if Cyprus joined NATO Turkey's ability to act would be severely curtailed and subject to delays.[19] This attachment to the Non-Aligned Movement was also highlighted by the fact that Makarios' first foreign trip after independence was not to Greece, as many had expected, but to Egypt to meet with President Nasser. In retrospect, it was hardly surprising that Makarios did not visit Athens. Prime Minister Karamanlis made it clear that it wished to have little to do with Cyprus now that the issue had been solved. The wider legacy of 1955-59 was twenty-five years of Greek-Turkish entente left in tatters – a process that had first been established by Venizelos and Ataturk in the late-1920s. Athens and Ankara now tried to push Cyprus into the political background.[20] In contrast, relations between London and Nicosia improved swiftly. Makarios appeared keen to strengthen ties with London now that independence had been achieved.[21] Arriving in Britain to attend the Commonwealth Heads of Government Conference, in March 1961, he stated:

> In spite of the differences and bitterness of the past, our relations with the United Kingdom are now very good. We shall do our utmost, in a spirit of goodwill, further to strengthen our relations with the UK as well as other participants in the Commonwealth...The past is forgotten.[22]

Meanwhile, although things were progressing well in terms of foreign policy, it was unclear how things would develop internally on the island. The Turkish Cypriots considered the political outcome of the Zurich-London Agreements to be neither extremely good nor extremely bad. Although they did not get thei wish for *Taksim* they had been spared *Enosis*.[23] The constitution had certainly given them a degree of influence that outweighed the actual size of their community. As 18% of the island's populace they were entitled to 30% of all civil service posts and 40% of all military posts. At the ministerial level they held three of the ten appointments including one of the three key ministries: finance,

---

19 Clerides, *op.cit.*, (Volume 1), p.124.
20 Woodhouse, *Modern Greece. A Short History*, p.280
21 Vassos Lyssarides, interview with the author.
22 *Keesing's Contemporary Archives*, March 18-25, 1961, p.17987.
23 Dodd (ed.) *The Political Social and Economic Development of Northern Cyprus*, p.6

foreign affairs or defence. They had also been given considerable autonomy. Two communal chambers had also been established that took responsibility for a large number of issues that were directly relevant to each community, such as religion and education.

In contrast to the Turkish Cypriots, most Greek Cypriots resented the new situation. EOKA had fought for *Enosis*, and many Greek Cypriots regarded independence with derision. The fact that this same independence had given the Turkish Cypriots a considerable, if not decisive, say over government, despite being such a small minority, made the enforced independence almost unbearable.[24] Key sources of resentment included the fact that the House of Representatives was forced to seek the agreement of the majority of both Greek Cypriot and Turkish Cypriot members before being able to pass legislation on fiscal, electoral or municipal matters and that all pieces of legislation and important government actions were open to veto by both the President and the Turkish Cypriot Vice-President of the Republic.

As a result, the Greek Cypriots soon became resentful of the political bind in which they found themselves. Plans were launched to change the situation, by force if necessary. A leading architect of this process was Polykarpos Yiorgadjis, a former senior leader of EOKA, and now Interior Minister, who drew up and circulated a secret document, the Akritas Plan, which outlined the exact measures that would be taken. Because of their influence in the Greek Cypriot community, Makarios had had to accept many of these figures into his government, including Yiorgadjis, if only to prevent them from expressing public opposition to the new order.[25] Additionally, Makarios continued to call for *Enosis*, even though this was explicitly banned under the constitution.[26]

By 1962, the situation had become unstable. The first real signs of major constitutional crisis arose with a dispute over the constitutional requirement for the establishment of separate Greek and Turkish municipalities in the five main towns Nicosia, Limassol, Famagusta, Larnaca, and Paphos. The Greek Cypriots argued that these provisions overlooked demographic and geographical realities and did not account for the fact that the two communities did not live in clearly defined areas away from one another. In an attempt to address the issue, Makarios offered Kuchuk a proposal to introduce unified municipalities with the benefit of safeguards to protect the rights of the Turkish Cypriots. Kuchuk made it clear that the separate municipalities had to be instituted before any such change could be made. Deadlock ensued and after more than a year of negotiations between the Turkish and Greek Cypriots over the issue, Makarios decided that the question could only be solved within the bounds of a range of constitutional amendments that would alter

24 Andreas Ziartides, in an interview with the author, noted that those on the right of the political spectrum generally felt these feelings more strongly. AKEL, although opposed to the Zurich Agreement on the grounds that it placed conditions on the independence of Cyprus and had brought the Turkish Army onto the island, nonetheless felt that it could be made to work.

25 Markides, *The Rise and Fall of the Cyprus Republic*, pp.87-88

26 A number of these statements can be found in Reddaway, *Burdened with Cyprus*, pp.192-194.

the balance of the relationship between the two communities and, in his opinion, enable the smoother running of the government.[27]

However, during his first visit to Ankara, in November that year, the Turkish Government explicitly warned Makarios that any attempt to alter the constitution would be treated by Turkey as a 'most serious matter'.[28] Makarios then approached the Greek Government, which advised the Archbishop to handle the matter extremely delicately. In a secret letter to Makarios in April 1963, the Greek Foreign Minister, Evangelos Averoff-Tositsas, stressed the real danger that any attempt to alter the 1960 agreements would lead to a breakdown in relations between the Greek and Turkish Cypriots and therefore pose the danger of a wider Greek-Turkish conflict.[29] Despite all the words of caution, the Archbishop was undeterred.

An opportunity to act came that summer when the government of Constantine Karamanlis fell. Makarios immediately got to work on drafting a final set of points to present to the Turkish Cypriots and the Guarantor Powers. As part of this effort he sought advice from Sir Frank Soskice, an eminent British lawyer who had been a minister in the post-war Attlee Government, on the legality of intervention by one of the Guarantor powers in response to such a change. Soskice argued that intervention would not be legal if articles of the Constitution were left unimplemented but that intervention would be justified if constitutional amendments were made that could have a substantive effect as regards the security of the Turkish Cypriots.[30] The advice seemed to make it clear that Makarios was engaging in a risky venture. Despite this view, Makarios had evidently made up his mind to act and proceeded to the next stage.

On 17 November, the Archbishop sent a copy of his proposed amendments to the British Prime Minister, Sir Alec Douglas-Home, for his inspection prior to officially submitting the plan to the Turkish Cypriots and the Guarantor Powers. Receiving no rejection or warning from London, on 29 November the Archbishop issued his plans for a 13-point amendment to the Constitution. The proposal included abolishing the veto of both the president and vice-president, limiting the range of legislation that needed to be passed by separate majorities, unifying the security forces and the judicial system, altering the structure and voting system of the Public Service Commission and abolishing the two communal chambers.[31]

These changes proved unacceptable to the Turkish Government, which officially rejected the ideas on 11 December. Despite assurances given by Makarios as to the

---

27 For a thorough account of this issue see Diana Weston Markides. *Cyprus 1957-63.*

28 Salahi R. Sonyel, "New Light on the Genesis of the Conflict: British Documents, 1960-67", pp.21-22.

29 English translation appearing in Clerides, *op. cit.*, (Volume 1), p.152

30 The exact details of the exchange between Glafcos Clerides, the President of the House of Representatives and Legal Adviser to Makarios, and Sir Frank Soskice can be found in Appendix F of Clerides, *op. cit.*, (Volume 1), pp.445-465. Osman Orek, the Minister of Defence at the time, claimed that Makarios had told him that Soskice's view was that the Treaties were not correct under the terms of the United Nations Charter. Osman Orek, interview with the author.

31 "Suggested Measures to Facilitate the Smooth Functioning of the State and Remove Certain Causes of Inter-Communal Friction", Salih, *op. cit.*, pp.132-143

intention of the amendments to facilitate a smoother working of the Constitution, the plans effectively wiped out Turkish Cypriot political power in the Republic of Cyprus. Almost immediately following Turkey's reaction there was a marked heightening of tensions on the island. On 19 December, Sir Arthur Clark, the British High Commissioner in Cyprus, visited the President of the Greek Cypriot Communal Chamber, Glafkos Clerides, on his way to the airport to depart for London. According to a memo submitted by Clerides to the Cypriot Government, Clark remarked on his personal regret that Turkey had been so hasty to reject the plan and stated the following view on the next stage of events:

> That in the event of clashes and fighting between the two sides, the use of the British forces in Cyprus to restore law and order was totally out of the question, for two reasons: firstly, the British forces in Cyprus were insufficient and would only be used to protect British nationals. Secondly, in the opinion of the British Government, the guarantors are not entitled to intervene in Cyprus without the consent of the Security Council, and this would take time.[32]

Two days later, fighting finally broke out between the Greek and Turkish Cypriots.

---

32 Clerides, *op. cit.*, (Volume 1), p.195

2

The Outbreak of Fighting

Tensions rose in Cyprus over the days following Turkey's rejection of the constitutional amendments and many expected disturbances to take place at any moment. *Halkin Sesi*, the leading Turkish language newspaper on the island, claimed that the Greek Cypriot leadership had instituted a number of measures to contain the Turkish Cypriot community in the event of any outbreak of fighting. For example, the paper claimed that the Greek Cypriots would establish a number of roadblocks, which would be used to seal off the Turkish Cypriot quarter of Nicosia. In an attempt to ensure that these procedures would be effective, the report said that the Greek Cypriots were conducting practice exercises at night within the old Venetian walls of Nicosia.[1] It was perhaps with this in mind that tempers flared in the early hours of 21 December 1963, when Greek Cypriot irregulars operating within the old Venetian walls of Nicosia demanded to see the identification papers of some Turkish Cypriots who were returning home from an evening out.[2] As word of the incident quickly spread Turkish Cypriot paramilitaries took to the streets. At around twenty past three in the morning gun shots were reported. By dawn two Turkish Cypriots were dead and eight others, both Greek and Turkish Cypriots, were wounded.[3]

As the day progressed there were numerous reports of sporadic gunfire around the old town as a large crowd of Turkish Cypriots, many armed, roamed the streets. Initial appeals for calm issued by President Makarios and Vice-President Kuchuk were ignored and by afternoon the fighting had spread to other parts of the capital. By the next morning, authorities in Larnaca were also reporting violent incidents. However, as evening approached the situation on the island appeared to be calming down. It was a short lived respite. Fighting erupted again the following morning when Greek Cypriot families living in the strategically important Nicosia suburb of Omorphita, which was primarily Turkish Cypriot, came under heavy attack. Soon afterwards conflict broke out in Famagusta when Turkish Cypriot gendarmes attempted to storm their headquarters. Likewise, fighting was reported from Kyrenia.

---

1 *Halkin Sesi*, 19 December 1963. When interviewed, Denktash maintained that the actual plan being worked on by the Greek Cypriots was an operation to surround the Turkish sector of Nicosia and 'finish off' the Turkish Cypriot leadership within twenty-four hours. At the same time Makarios intended to abrogate the Treaties and present a new set of moderate Turkish Cypriot leaders.

2 *Cyprus Mail*, 22 December 1963

3 *Ibid.*

The Guarantor Powers become involved

By now the situation was clearly spiralling out of control and the Guarantor Powers were starting to worry. Although the Cypriot Foreign Minister, Spyros Kyprianou, who was in London for a scheduled meeting of the Guarantor Powers, said on 23 December that the United Kingdom regarded the matter as being an 'internal affair',[4] by the next day the British Government's view had changed. Kyprianou was invited to the Commonwealth Office to discuss the events in the island with Duncan Sandys, the Commonwealth Secretary, Sir Arthur Clark and the Duke of Devonshire, the Minister of State.[5] In Ankara, the Turkish Foreign Minister, Feridun Erkin, held meetings with the US Ambassador, Raymond Hare, and the Soviet Ambassador, Nikita Ryzhov. Following the breakdown of another ceasefire in Nicosia the three governments issued a joint appeal to the two communities to stop fighting and offered their good offices as a means of resolving the causes of the crisis. However, this had little effect and the next day, Christmas Day, Turkey ordered three fighter aircraft to fly at low level over Nicosia. As this was happening Greek and Turkish Cypriots forces again clashed near the strategically important Kyrenia road, this time around the village of Gunyeli.

With little remaining hope that the fighting would subside, Prime Minister Douglas-Home flew back to London from his Scottish residence and ordered an emergency cabinet meeting. During the discussions, it was agreed that Britain's prime concern was the protection of the Sovereign Base Areas and the fifteen thousand British nationals, mainly attached to the military, who resided outside of the Bases.[6] Although it was pointed out that British citizens could be withdrawn into the Bases or even evacuated, plans for which had been drawn up,[7] it was quickly recognised that a policy of sealing off the Bases would not work. Apart from still leaving them at risk from fighting, the Bases relied on the Republic for manpower and resources. Prolonged and serious fighting outside would naturally affect local staff and the provision of supplies and would therefore jeopardise the ability of the Bases to function.[8] Additionally, it was pointed out that any major change in the balance of power on the island in favour of the Greek Cypriots could lead to political, or even military, attacks on the British Bases.[9] Under these circumstances it therefore seemed logical to use Britain's military forces on the island to forestall any further fighting. By taking a more active approach to the problem London believed that it would be able to protect the delicate balance of power on the island, which would in turn protect the political foundations upon which the Bases existed. However, the cabinet also discussed the obvious wider concern that if something was not done quickly to halt the fighting the other two Guarantor Powers, Greece and Turkey, might chose to become involved.[10]

---

4 *Cyprus Mail*, 24 December 1963
5 *Ibid.*, 25 December 1963
6 The actual figure was cited as 15,661 – *FO 371/168983*
7 *FO 371/168983*
8 Anthony Verrier, "Cyprus: Britain's Security Role", *The World Today*, March 1964, p.132
9 *Ibid.*, p.132
10 'CYPRUS: Memorandum by the Prime Minister', 2 January 1964, *CAB 129/116*

The dangers of the conflict spreading beyond the island were already becoming clear. In Turkey, public opinion was increasingly in favour of intervention and there had been a number of large-scale student demonstrations calling for military action. Soon afterwards reports emerged that there had been a rise in activity in and around many army and naval bases, which seemed to indicate that a general mobilisation was about to occur.[11] Despite its steps to ready for a unilateral intervention, the Turkish Government was nonetheless aware that any direct action could well lead to a full-scale war with Greece. It was therefore felt that a joint intervention would be a better course of action and a proposal for joint action by the Guarantor Powers was announced by the Turkish Government following a meeting between Prime Minister Inonu, the Chief of the General Staff, General Cevdet Sunay, and several other senior military commanders. However, the group decided to continue planning for a unilateral intervention in case the tripartite plan failed.[12]

Ankara had little to fear. A similar view of the situation had been reached in Athens after a meeting of the Supreme Defence Council that had been chaired by Crown Prince Constantine, who was deputising for the ailing King Paul.[13] Unlike Turkey, Greece was under very little domestic pressure to take the first step. Instead Athens was concerned about a Turkish intervention, which would necessarily require a Greek response. Such a strike and counter-strike could quickly lead to a full-scale war between the two countries. Moreover, rumours of an imminent Turkish invasion, which had emerged after Turkish warships were sighted off the coast of Cyprus, no doubt helped to force a quick decision to support joint action from Greece, which noted its concern about Turkish moves to the US and British ambassadors.[14] Thus, Athens also decided that a joint intervention was the best hope to restore peace on the island and avert a wider regional conflict. As the British Prime Minister, Sir Alec Douglas-Home, noted of the situation:

> When it became clear that this appeal had failed, the three Guaranteeing Powers, on 25th December, informed the Government of Cyprus of their readiness to intervene, if invited to do so, to restore order, by means of a Joint Intervention Force, under British command, and composed of the forces of the United Kingdom, Greece and Turkey stationed in Cyprus.[15]

Archbishop Makarios accepts Guarantor Power intervention

Although tripartite intervention had been agreed by London, Ankara and Athens, and had been put to the Cypriot Government in unison, Makarios refused to agree to the plan immediately as he wanted to think it through. He only had a short time to do so. By the following day, 26 December, another surge in fighting meant that an answer could not be

11 Athens to FO, No.832, 30 December 1963, *FO 371/168984*
12 *Cyprus Mail*, 27 December 1963
13 *Ibid.* King Paul died just a few months later, on 6 March 1964.
14 *The New York Times*, 23/12/63, p.3
15 'CYPRUS: Memorandum by the Prime Minister', 2 January 1964, *CAB 129/116*

delayed any longer. Turkey was becoming more agitated and was actively preparing its troops for unilateral military action, a point stressed to Makarios by the British military attaché.[16] The Archbishop therefore finally accepted, in principle, that some form of tripartite intervention was necessary.[17] However he insisted on one important condition. Command of the force would be in the hands of a British officer, rather a Greek or Turk.[18] This was accepted by the three Guarantors and it was announced that the force would be led by Major-General Peter Young, the General Officer Commanding (GOC) Cyprus District. His deputy would be Group Captain Campbell, the Commander of RAF Nicosia, who would take responsibility for liaising with Colonels Tzouvelekis and Evsoz, the commanders of the Greek and Turkish contingents to the force, both of whom were considered to be moderate and had, prior to the outbreak of fighting, ensured that relations between their two contingents had been cordial.[19]

At this point the force ran into its first problem. Neither the Greek nor the Turkish contingents were in their camps.[20] The Turkish troop contingent had withdrawn from their barracks on Christmas day[21] and Turkish soldiers had been assisting the Turkish Cypriots fortify their positions. More worryingly, the contingent had fought directly with Greek Cypriots forces around the village of Ortakoy to the north of Nicosia.[22] The Greek contingent had also left its barracks and had taken part in clashes but, following notification of Makarios' approval for joint intervention, it had returned to its camp.[23] The trouble was that the Greek Government would not allow its troops to participate without a corresponding Turkish presence. However, with just hours before the start of the joint action only a few senior Turkish officers were available to take up duties. Moreover, in spite clear orders to accept the authority of General Young, the commander of the Turkish contingent pointedly refused to act on any command without specific permission from Ankara.[24] Under these circumstances it was obvious that the new force would begin its duties comprised solely of British troops.

The Joint Truce Force begins operations

Despite this drawback in the early hours of the morning of 27 December the first British units serving in what was called the 'Joint Truce Force' left their bases to take up their positions in Nicosia. In addition to widespread newspaper coverage of the start of the operation, throughout the morning an announcement was broadcast, in Greek, every fifteen minutes on the state radio station stating:

---

16 Osman Orek, interview with the author.
17 *Cyprus Mail*, 29 December 1963
18 CRO to Nicosia, No.1093, 26 December 1963, *FO 371/168983*
19 Harbottle, *The Impartial Soldier*, p.15
20 *Cyprus Mail*, 27 December 1963
21 FO to Ankara, No.2162, 25 December 1963, *FO 371/168982*
22 Osman Orek, interview with the author.
23 Christodoulos Veniamin, interview with the author.
24 Nicosia to CRO, No.1095, 27 December 1963, *FO 371/168984*

> General Young, commanding forces which will assist the Government of [the] Republic in its efforts to preserve the cease fire and restore peace had a meeting with His Beatitude and Minister of Interior late last night when views [were] exchanged on best way to deal with situation. [It was] Agreed that forces under General's command will start patrolling in certain areas today. The public is called upon to be helpful so that task of forces assisting in restoration of law and order may effectively be achieved.[25]

Within hours British units had taken up their positions in the city. At the same time, a British medical team entered the Turkish Cypriot quarter of Nicosia to treat the several hundred who had been wounded during the previous six days of fighting.[26] As a result of the Truce Force's deployment the situation on the island had rapidly improved. Although there were still reports of a number of sporadic incidents of firing, and that Greek irregulars were continuing to fortify positions that had earlier been abandoned, there was nonetheless a feeling of optimism detectable in British communications back to London.[27] The following day General Young gave his first assessment of the situation:

> Except for one or two regrettable incidents today, the overall situation has greatly improved...The Greek Cypriot side have moved out of certain areas and British troops are now located in these positions...Further posts will be taken over tomorrow as part of a general measure for the relaxation of tension.[28]

The success of the operation was also stressed in Turkey by Prime Minister Inonu, much to the relief of all concerned, including the political establishment in Greece.[29] Indeed, the leader of the opposition, George Papandreou, even went as far as to send a message of appreciation to Ankara for having made this statement,[30] and voiced his thanks to the British Government for having taken on the responsibility for peacekeeping.[31] In addition, the Greek Cypriot leadership had accepted the military value of the British action. Indeed, within a day of the British troops having begun their operation, the Greek Cypriots stated that they, 'considered the first days activity as designed by Commander Joint Forces was excellent and they would like to see a gradual enlargement of the patrol activity based on the first days pattern.'[32]

---

25 Nicosia to CRO, No.1084, 27 December 1963, *FO 371/168984*
26 *The New York Times*, 27 December 1963
27 Nicosia to CRO, No.1095, 27 December 1963, *FO 371/168984*
28 *Cyprus Mail*, 29 December 1963
29 *The New York Times*, 28 December 1963
30 Athens to FO, No.829, 29 December 1963, *FO 371/168984*
31 Athens to FO, No.812, 28 December 1963, *FO 371/168981*. *Mesimvrini*, 28 December 1963
32 Nicosia to CRO, No.1101, 28 December 1963, *FO 371/168984*

Although the Greek Government was pleased with this success,[33] and had called upon the Greek media to be accurate in their reporting of events so as not to rouse public opinion,[34] the danger was already being expressed in Athens that without the participation of the Turkish forces continued Greek political support for the operation would be cast into doubt. With this in mind it was decided that any remaining Turkish and Greek troops either available, or able, would act as liaisons officers and interpreters between the Truce Force, combatants, and civilians. At the same time, members of the Greek and Turkish contingents were utilised as part of a tripartite field mediating team that was set up under the leadership of Commander Martin Packard, a British naval officer.[35] All these steps finally led to the partial integration of Greek and Turkish troops into the Joint Truce Force, although this was, as stated above, only at the liaison level. However, even with this improvement, there was no room for complacency. The continued dangers of the situation were made clear to the British troops that same day when they came under fire from Turkish Cypriots. No injuries were reported.

The first UN Security Council debate

Of greater concern, however, were the reports from the Royal Air Force that Turkish warships had been spotted just 15-20 miles off the Cyprus coast, sightings that had been reported this to the Greek Cypriots.[36] In response to the reported Turkish military build-up, the Greek Cypriots decided to take the matter to the United Nations Security Council. At four o'clock in the morning of 28 December 1963, the Cypriot Permanent Representative at the United Nations, Zenon Rossides, addressed a letter to Francis Plimpton, the deputy US deputy representative at the UN, who held the post of President of the Security Council in December 1963, complaining about the, 'intervention in the internal affairs of Cyprus by the threat and use of force against its territorial integrity and political independence.'[37]

Upon hearing about the move, the Turkish Foreign Minister, Feridun Erkin, summoned the British Ambassador, Sir Denis Allen, to his office where he made it clear that the letter was at odds with Turkey's position as one of the three 'powers' that had been invited by the Cyprus Government to restore order. He therefore asked the British Government to use whatever influence it may have with the Cypriot Government to withdraw the letter. If this were not possible, Erkin made it clear that he hoped that no meeting would take place. Instead, the Turkish Government would be prepared to answer

---

33 Athens to FO, No.828, 28 December 1963, *FO 371/168983*

34 Athens to FO, No.826, 29 December 1963, *FO 371/168891*

35 For more information about this effort see Packard, "Cyprus 1964: Subversion of a Mission".

36 FO to Ankara, No.2247, 27 December 1963, *FO 371/168984*

37 *United Nations Security Council Document*, S/5488, 28 December 1963. Clerides claimed that Rossides was acting on his own initiative, Clerides, *Cyprus. My Deposition* (Volume 2), p.21. However, one former diplomat, speaking on condition of anonymity, stated that Rossides was particularly close to Makarios and could call him directly at any time. It was suggested that Makarios may therefore have actually agreed to this step directly with Rossides without informing Clerides.

Rossides in writing.[38] Although London was at first unsure whether Erkin was telling the truth about his government's intentions and wanted Turkey to issue an urgent statement of reassurance regarding its actions,[39] reports soon emerged that showed that the Turkish naval vessels were no longer in a threatening position.[40] Armed with this news, a British official approached the Cypriot Foreign Minister, Spyros Kyprianou, in an attempt to have him call off the Security Council meeting. Kyprianou, however, seemed to believe that it was too late to do this.[41] London therefore informed Sir Patrick Dean, Britain's Permanent Representative at the UN, that if the matter came before the Security Council his position '...should be that there is no (repeat no) evidence that the Turkish naval force is making for Cyprus. There is a Turkish port at Iskenderun and ships making for there would have to pass close to Cypriot coast.'[42]

As requested by the Greek Cypriots, a meeting was eventually convened that evening. It proved to be a short discussion. At the start of the session, the Turkish permanent representative at the United Nations, Adnan Kural, denied that Turkey had any aggressive intent. Furthermore, the fact that the vessels in question were travelling away from Cyprus seems to have convinced the Council that there was little to worry about at this stage. The meeting was therefore adjourned without producing any specific plan of action, despite the fact that Greece had by now placed its navy on a four-hour alert in response to the reports.[43]

First discussions about UN peacekeeping

The Security Council debate was not the first attempt made by Rossides to involve the United Nations. A few days earlier he had held discussions with the UN Secretary-General, U Thant, with a view to forming a United Nations peacekeeping force. In a report sent to London by Sir Patrick Dean, the British Permanent Representative to the Organisation, the main points of the conversation were cited as follows:

> Rossides' first proposal was that a contingent from UNEF should be transferred to Cyprus. U Thant had told him that this was quite impossible. UNEF had a particular mandate and the troops could not be transferred elsewhere without (gp undec) [sic] authority and it was in any case very unlikely that those countries from which the contingents were drawn would agree. Rossides appeared to accept this, but then suggested a United Nations presence. U Thant told him that this could take one of two forms, either something on the lines of the Graham Mission in Kashmir following a Security Council resolution, or a presence like that of Spinelli in Yemen, which had been made possible after informal consultation with

38 Ankara to FO, No.1425, 27 December 1963, *FO 371/168984*
39 Washington to FO, No.4078, 28 December 1963, *FO 371/168984*
40 Nicosia to FO, No.1098, 28 (Cyprus), 27 (London) December 1963, *FO 371/168984*
41 Nicosia to CRO, No.1103, 28 December 1963, *FO 371/168984*
42 FO to UKMIS UN New York, No.5130, 28 December, *FO 371/168984*
43 *Cyprus Mail*, 29 December 1963

> members of the Security Council but mainly because the parties concerned were prepared to meet the cost...U Thant had then asked Rossides what the United Nations representative would be supposed to do. Rossides had in mind that he should study the constitution and presumably report on its implementation. He had been told, however, that this, too, was quite impossible and that the most a United Nations representative could properly do would be to observe the general situation and report to the Secretary General...U Thant told me at the end of our discussion that he personally was against the whole idea of United Nations involvement, and it was very hard to see what useful purpose it would serve.[44]

Similarly, the British Government had also examined this idea for some form UN peacekeeping. On the very day that the Joint Truce Force took up positions, a telegram was sent by the Foreign Office to Ankara that noted that while tripartite intervention might succeed the question of disengagement from peacekeeping duties would have to be addressed as soon as possible.[45] The need to consider disengagement was no doubt affected by the large number of newspaper editorials across the political spectrum that saw British involvement in the Cyprus Crisis as being either dangerous or without merit.[46] For those that accepted the need for peacekeeping, calls were made to replace the Truce Force with a United Nations' force.[47] However, London quickly decided that UN involvement was unsuitable for a variety of reasons:

> (a.) Experience of the Congo suggests that the despatch of United Nations military contingents might have unfortunate consequences. Observers might be another matter;
> (b.) We would lose virtually all control over future developments. Hitherto our position as the neutral among the three Guaranteeing Powers has given us considerable influence;
> (c.) The United Nations may start suggestions that our occupation of the Sovereign Base Areas is undesirable and has a disturbing effect. The Afro-Asian element in the United Nations would probably seize any opportunity which might arise to try to oust us altogether from the island;
> (d.) The Turkish government would almost certainly be opposed to any invitation to the United Nations. In view of the fact of the Greek majority on the island and of the fact that they enjoy much better contacts in United Nations circles, the Turks would almost certainly regard any United Nations initiative as most unlikely to favour the Turkish community.[48]

---

44 UKMIS UN New York to FO, No.2346, 27 December 1963, *FO 371/168983*
45 FO to Ankara, No.2237, 27 December 1963, *FO 371/168983*
46 For example, *Daily Express*, 27 December 1963
47 *The Guardian*, the *Daily Herald*, and the *Daily Mail*, 27 December 1963
48 FO to Ankara, No.2237, 27 December 1963, *FO 371/168983*

However, the Government's public opposition to a United Nations presence was stated in somewhat different terms to these behind the scenes objections; as became clear in an exchange of letters that took place at the time between the Labour MP Tom Driberg and the Foreign Secretary, R.A. Butler. On 29 December Driberg wrote to Butler stating his view that while it was 'natural and inevitable' that British troops should be called upon to assist, in the case that the emergency should continue some form of UN presence should be organised that would draw on contingents from countries that had not been involved with Cyprus over the previous years. Moreover, he stressed that he did not see why, 'our troops should sustain further losses and attract the odium so lavishly available in Cyprus.'[49]

In reply, Lord Carrington, writing on behalf of Butler, presented the public opposition to the plan by the Government. He started his letter by accepting that peacekeeping on the island was indeed a 'thankless task' and did run the risk of attracting opposition from both communities. However, he stressed that their presence had prevented a full-scale conflict from erupting between the two communities, which would have been backed by Greece and Turkey, and that British troops would probably be needed for a while until such time that an alternative force could be put in place. As far as some form of UN involvement was concerned, Carrington explained that the UN Charter allowed for regional attempts to solve efforts before they were put to the Security Council, but that the British Government had nonetheless considered ways in which to involve the United Nations. Regarding specific UN peacekeeping, the opposition of the Secretary-General was invoked as the main reason why it was not being considered at this stage. The fact that the Security Council had also opted to avoid taking a position on the matter only served to strengthen the view that the United Nations wished to steer clear of the problem at this stage.[50] On a final note, Carrington stressed that any major debate could only help to exacerbate tensions between Greece and Turkey, and therefore between the two communities, which would in turn threaten the 'uneasy' peace that had developed.[51]

Renewed fears of Turkish intervention

Although the Turkish Government had denied that it was preparing for an intervention, in the days following the Security Council debate a number of telegrams were sent to London indicating a Turkish mobilisation.[52] Apparently realising Britain's concern, Ankara assured Britain that it was only conducting precautionary military build-ups in Iskenderun that were solely aimed at providing 'moral support' for the Turkish Cypriots, and that it was not necessarily planning a military intervention.[53]

Interestingly, the British Government was unsure whether it should trust these assurances. They had good reason to believe that Turkey was in fact planning to take

---

49 Letter from Tom Driberg MP to the Foreign Secretary, 29 December 1963, *FO 371/168981*

50 *Sunday Times*, 29 December 1963

51 Letter from Lord Carrington to Tom Driberg MP, 2 January 1964, *FO 371/168981*

52 'Cyprus: Build-up of Turkish Forces; possibility of invasion', *FO 371/168983*

53 FO to Ankara, No. 2313, 30 December 1963, *FO 371/168983*

action. During a meeting between Sir Denis Allen and Foreign Minister Erkin in Ankara, on 29 December, the Turkish Foreign Minister raised the question as to whether an action taken by one of the Guarantor Powers in Cyprus would have to be opposed by another.[54] In particular he argued that the provisions of the Treaty of Guarantee meant that an intervention staged by one Guarantor Power should not be opposed by another. Although stressing that under the current situations the question was not of immediate concern, the Turkish Foreign Minister nonetheless asked for clarification on the British Government's view on this point, and hoped that there would be agreement between the two of them on this matter. Suitably worried by this conversation, Allen immediately contacted London for advice.

Responding to the question, the High Commission in Nicosia pointed out that the Turkish view was 'absurd'.[55] If this was truly the case, or so the view from the British diplomats in Nicosia ran, then one party's intervention would deprive the other two Guarantors from intervening. Under these circumstances, the natural reaction would be to gain 'unjustifiable advantage' by intervening first, even before the possibilities for joint action had been explored, and thereby prevent the others from acting.

Fearful of the implications of Erkin's comments London ordered that all further communications with the Turkish Government would be handled solely through the Foreign Office, and not jointly with the Commonwealth Relations Office. Furthermore, a decision was taken to inform the Turkish Government the Britain would be ready to talk on the Cyprus issue with both the Greek and Turkish Governments at any time, day or night.[56]

---

54 Ankara to FO, No.1444, 29 December 1963, *FO 371/168981*

55 Nicosia to CRO, No.214, 1 January 1964, *FO 371/168981*

56 *FO 371/168981*

3

Initial Peacemaking Efforts

On 28 December the British Commonwealth Secretary, Duncan Sandys, arrived on the island to add political weight to General Young's peacekeeping efforts. Following a series of separate meetings with President Makarios and Vice-President Kuchuk, and with the Greek and Turkish Ambassadors, Sandys announced the formation of a political liaison committee tasked with facilitating ceasefire agreements and ensuring future cooperation between the Truce Force, Greek and Turkish army contingents, and the Greek and Turkish Cypriots.[1] Following further discussions, this time with the Greek and Turkish Cypriot military commanders, he also managed to gain the official, and working, acceptance for the creation of an officially recognised ceasefire line manned by British troops.

The next morning the new liaison committee held its first meeting at the residence of the British High Commissioner, just within the Turkish quarter of the city. Following twelve hours of talks the committee produced a seven-point plan:[2]

1. Arrangements to ensure the complete freedom of movement of British patrols in both sectors of Nicosia.
2. The withdrawal of Greek and Turkish Cypriot fighters from strong points on either side of the cease-fire line and their replacement by British troops. Thereby creating a neutral zone.
3. Arrangements for the removal of Turkish dead and wounded from the Omorphita area.
4. The exchange of refugees and hostages by both sides.
5. The re-establishment of the telephone system between Nicosia and Kyrenia, thought to have been cut by Turkish Cypriots.
6. The re-establishment of postal services in the Turkish sector of Nicosia.

---

1 Nicosia to CRO, No.1114, 29 December 1963, *FO 371/168985*. The Committee it would be made up of the Greek and Turkish Ambassadors, Delivanis and Ozkol. For the Greek Cypriots the President of the House of Representatives, Glafkos Clerides, and a Greek Cypriot Minister, Polykarpos Yiorgadjis, would participate. For the Turkish Cypriots Osman Orek, the Minister of Defence, Rauf R. Denktash, the President of the Turkish Cypriot Communal Chamber, and Halit Ali Riza, a member of the House of Representatives would be present. Furthermore, General Young and the commanders of the Greek and Turkish contingents were also invited to play a role. It was also decided that Sandys would chair the first meeting personally, but that later sessions would be chaired by Cyril Pickard, an official from the Commonwealth Relations Office who would serve as Acting British High Commissioner in place of Sir Arthur Clark, who was very ill.

2 *Keesing's Contemporary Archives*, June 13-20, 1964, p.20113

> 7. The possibility of restarting Turkish broadcasts, and steps to secure more objective presentation of news in both languages.

This agreement was quickly put into effect and the Truce Force was able to supervise the exchange of a large number of hostages in Nicosia. A few days later, on 3 January, Turkish Cypriot forces released another thirteen Greeks.[3]

In light of the Truce Force's success in reducing tensions on the island another attempt was made to try to induce the Turkish contingent to return to barracks and accept the command of General Young. After a meeting in Ankara between Erkin, Inonu, and General Sunay, the Turkish Government sent a telegram to Sandys assuring him that the Turkish forces on the island had been told to accept orders form General Young and that they would relinquish their positions once the British could step in and take control of the areas that had been vacated.[4] On the basis of this telegram, London decided to reinforce its presence on the island. However, it was not a straightforward decision to take. Already there were concerns that any further increase in troop numbers would have to draw on forces from the British Army of the Rhine (BAOR), and that any larger force in Cyprus would create problems regarding continued British commitments in both Aden and Malaysian Borneo.[5]

The attempt to abrogate the Treaty of Guarantee

By now it was clear that there could be no reduction of the British presence in Cyprus until the overall political situation was addressed. The two sides would have to talk. As if to emphasize the need for dialogue, a potentially dangerous situation developed when, on the evening of the 30 December, Foreign Minister Kyprianou laid out a three-point plan for future Greek and Turkish Cypriot relations. First of all he made it clear that the majority must rule. Secondly, there should be safeguards for the minority. Thirdly, and perhaps most controversially, the treaty links with Greece and Turkey should be cut and formal ties should remain with the United Kingdom alone.[6] The continued link with Britain was justified on the basis that Cyprus, as a member of the Commonwealth, should naturally look to the United Kingdom as the organisation's 'the leading country.'[7]

This last idea had first been put forward by Kyprianou during a meeting with the Duke of Devonshire in London on 23 December 1963, but judging from the lack of any follow-up documentation, the proposal appears to have not been taken seriously.[8] This time, however, Makarios had suggested the idea personally. Britain quickly rejected the plan on the grounds that this arrangement would inevitably leave it in the 'unsatisfactory' position of having to intervene alone between the communities to protect law and lives. Moreover, the

---

3 *Keesing's Contemporary Archives*, June 13-20, 1964, p.20113
4 Ankara to FO, No.1458, 30 December 1963, *FO 371/168984*
5 See *Keesing's Contemporary Archives*, July 18-25, 1964, p.20181
6 *Cyprus Mail*, 31 December 1963
7 *Ibid.*
8 'Cypriot Greek Proposal for a Bilateral Treaty with Britain', 6 January 1964, *FO 371/174745*

proposal would be unacceptable to Turkey, which would be concerned about Britain's longer-term ability to conduct such operations and might even be see London's acceptance of the proposal as evidence of partiality towards the Greek Cypriots.[9] Despite Britain's rejection of an alternative bilateral treaty, Makarios was obviously intent on abrogating the Treaty of Guarantee. He therefore sent a telegram to the world's heads of state, except those of the three Guarantor Powers (Greece had apparently already accepted the idea[10]), announcing his decision to terminate the agreement. On receiving the news, Sandys immediately went to see the Archbishop and told him that if he were serious about the plan he would have to bear the consequences for the Turkish reaction. Following a two hour meeting, Makarios backed down. A diplomatic face-saving statement was soon released clarifying that due to a translation error from the Greek the term 'abrogate' should have read: 'desire to secure the termination of these Treaties by appropriate means'. A crisis was averted.

The Turkish contingent remains in the field

Despite assurances given to Sandys by the Turkish Government that its forces on the island would report for duty, they had still failed to return to barracks. Fed up with London's failure to handle the matter by diplomatic means, the Greek Government informed the British Military Attaché that if the Turkish contingent were not forced to come under British command then the Greek contingent would no longer obey General Young.[11] As the later retraction of the threat by General Ioannis Pipilis, the Chief of Staff, showed such talk was driven more out of frustration than any real intent. This basic desire to co-operate was again proven soon afterwards when the Greek Government cooperated fully with the British Government on the question of the scheduled relief of Greek soldiers serving with the Greek contingent in Cyprus. This operation, which was originally due to have taken place at the end of December, had initially been delayed following British concerns that it may be interpreted by both the Turkish Cypriots as well as the Turkish Government as being a ploy by which to bolster the Greek military presence on the island.[12]

Fortunately, it seems as though London appreciated that the tough Greek stand on the issue was driven more by the demands of public opinion than by any wish to be obstructive or difficult. Hoping to see a continuation of the good working relationship that had developed, the British Government arranged a full briefing on Cyprus for the incoming caretaker government of Greece, which had just been created under the Deputy Governor of the Bank of Greece, John Paraskevopoulos, and was to be sworn in on 31 December.[13]

In contrast to the position adopted by Athens, the Greek Cypriots were proving to be less willing to accept the United Kingdom's caution on the issue of the continuing absence

9 'Note of a talk with Mr. Kyprianou on 20th January 1964', *FO 371/174745*
10 Athens to FO, No.814, 28 December 1963, *FO 371/168984*
11 Telegram from Athens to FO, No.833, 31 December 1963, *FO 371/168984*
12 Nicosia to Athens, No.9 and No.10, 1 January 1964, *FO 371/168981*
13 Athens to FO, No.833, 31 December 1963, *FO 371/168984*

of the Turkish contingent from their camp and they issued a statement alleging that the Turkish contingent was simply disregarding the orders of General Young by remaining placed outside of their barracks.[14] In reply to these claims, which caused outrage in Ankara, General Young sent a diplomatically phrased letter directly to the commander of the Turkish contingent assuring him that the views expressed did not represent his own position and that the claims had not been made in collusion with the Greek Cypriots:

> Makarios has made a statement to the effect that you declined to obey my orders. I would like you to know that the statement is completely in conflict with the truth. Today I assured our Ambassador in Ankara that with you I have been working in complete cooperation.[15]

Attempts at peacemaking

By this stage Nicosia was effectively divided with the Turkish Cypriots in the northern part of the capital and the Greek Cypriots in the south of the city. In a highly destabilising move, Kuchuk announced that the constitution was dead and that any further Greek and Turkish Cypriot cohabitation was impossible.[16] Regardless of the rhetoric, in reality the two sides would have to come together to discuss the political situation. The British Government therefore proposed holding a peace conference at which all the issues would be tackled. The idea for a conference seems to have been first articulated at the time when the Joint Truce Force took up duties,[17] but it was not until Sandys arrived on the island that the idea was formally presented to the two communities. It was suggested that London would be the best venue for such a conference, a location that was particularly favoured by the Turkish Government in light of the tensions on the island itself.[18]

Despite the comments of Kuchuk, the Turkish Cypriots accepted almost immediately on the condition that only five parties attend the conference – the United Kingdom, Greece, Turkey, and the two Cypriot communities.[19] Sandys seemingly agreed to accept this.[20] The Commonwealth Secretary then approached the Greek Cypriots. Makarios, as had been the case with the request to establish a peacekeeping force, was unwilling to give an answer then and there, even though the Turkish Cypriots had agreed. Indeed, the Archbishop only gave his final acceptance of the offer just minutes before Sandys departed from the island, on 2 January, at the end of his five-day peacemaking mission.[21]

---

14 UKDEL NATO Paris to FO, No.10, 6 January 1964, *FO 371/168984*
15 UKDEL NATO Paris to FO, No.10, 6 January 1964, *FO 371/168984*
16 *The New York Times*, 31 December 1963
17 FO to Ankara, No.2237, 27 December 1963, *FO 371/168983*
18 Ankara to FO, No.1434, 28 December 1963, *FO 371/168983*
19 Osman Orek, interview with the author.
20 Osman Orek, interview with the author. Orek insisted that Sandys confirm this promise in writing and sign under the text. Sandys did so, but underneath wrote: 'Good luck to you'. In the view of Orek this meant that it would be the responsibility of the Turkish Cypriots to enforce this 'promise'.
21 Clerides, *op. cit.*, (Volume 1), p.230

The following day, Makarios gave his first press conference since the outbreak of violence thirteen days earlier. As expected, the questions mainly focussed on the likely approach the Greek Cypriots would take in London. Despite adopting a generally positive view about the prospect for peace, Makarios nonetheless made it clear that if the London Conference failed he would again bring Cyprus to attention of the United Nations.[22]

Peacekeeping efforts continue

By now the all the British troops detailed to serve with the Truce Force had arrived on the island. Following fifty nine transport sorties since 26 December, there were now several thousand soldiers in Cyprus – including two hundred and fifty army technicians and a number of helicopters. According to the Ministry of Defence, 'no further moves were contemplated so long as situation remained calm.'[23]

Within Nicosia the Truce Force continued to keep a close watch on the situation by being, as *The Times* put it, 'out on foot, patrolling roads and showing the uniform at important junctions and roofs.'[24] At the same time, General Young had now established in his headquarters on the top floor of the Cornaro hotel on the outskirts of the city. Meanwhile, the Truce Force continued trying to ensure that the general island wide ceasefire was being observed and British troops with the aid of a number of jeeps, twenty armoured cars, and four helicopters began to collect information on the conditions in a number of Turkish Cypriot and mixed villages. Additionally, the force supervised a meeting between Greek and Turkish community leaders in Larnaca and Famagusta. In Famagusta this led to a return to normality following a few skirmishes that had disrupted the otherwise good communal relations in the city.[25] In Kyrenia a serious clash between Greek and Turkish Cypriots was averted by the direct intervention of an RAF patrol.

Despite its success, or because of it, the Truce Force was soon criticised by certain elements of the Greek Cypriot community for taking too neutral a role and not protecting those Turkish Cypriots who had remained loyal to the Government.[26] Luckily, such reports did not seem to result in any backlash against the Truce Force, which maintained its position in a number of places. Indeed, General Young noted the way in which the widened area of the Force's operations was leading to greater freedom of movement and that food and medical supplies were now being distributed to areas of need.[27] In order to meet these demands for food the Greek Cypriots went so far as to allow a number of Turkish warships to dock at Famagusta where, under the auspices of the Truce Force and Greek Cypriot police, they brought several large consignments of aid for the Turkish Cypriots.[28]

22 *Cyprus Mail*, 4 January 1964
23 *The Times*, 4 January 1964
24 *Ibid.*
25 *Cyprus Mail*, 8 January 1964
26 *Eleftheria* and *Haravghi*, 8 January 1964
27 *Cyprus Mail*, 10 January 1964
28 *Ibid.*, 14 January 1964

The spectre of partition

While most of the Turkish Cypriot leadership viewed the Joint Truce Force favourably,[29] almost all remained firmly of the opinion that Turkey remained their ultimate guardian.[30] Some sections of the Turkish Cypriot leadership, as was the case in parts of the Greek Cypriot community, viewed the Force as a temporary measure. For example, on 8 January, Rauf Denktash stated that, 'we hope [the Truce Force] will hold the line while the talks are on but we do not visualise them staying forever.'[31] However, rather than seeing the Force leave as part of an agreed political settlement with the Greek Cypriots, suspicions were growing that the Turkish Cypriot leadership were actively engaged in trying to realise their old political aim of *Taksim* (partition). This suspicion was no doubt fanned by the fact that following the first outbreak of communal violence on 21 December, almost all of the Turkish Cypriots civil servants in Nicosia had withdrawn from their government posts by midday on 22 December. Furthermore, the Turkish Cypriots had started to congregate into enclaves in a number of locations. In one case, near the town of Lefka, west of Nicosia, it was claimed that six thousand Turkish Cypriots, one thousand of whom were refugees, were massed in an area of just four square miles.[32]

Over the years there has been a strong debate about whether the violence that occurred in December 1963 was engineered by one or other community in an attempt to achieve wider political aims. While there has been a tendency to view Makarios's proposal for an amendment to the constitution as the final manifest cause of the communal fighting, the evidence seems to suggest that both communities had been engaged in a gradual process of building up arms supplies since the first days of the Republic of Cyprus in the hope that they would have a chance to enforce their political aims.[33] The Akritas Plan was just the one side of the coin. At the same time as many Greek Cypriots were still working to achieve *Enosis*, it appears that certain elements of the Turkish Cypriot community had continued to plan for *Taksim*.[34] However, while the communal fighting helped strengthen

29 Rauf R. Denktash, Necati Ertekun and Osman Orek, interviews with the author.

30 Rauf R. Denktash, interview with the author.

31 *Cyprus Mail*, 9 January 1964

32 *Keesing's Contemporary Archives*, June 13-20, 1964, p.20113

33 Almost everyone the author spoke to from both communities seemed to accept the fact that there had been a significant amount of arms stored at the end of the EOKA period, as well as significant amounts of arms imported in the post-independence period. Interestingly, many of those interviewed claimed that the arms build up had actually been conducted by the 'other' community, and that their own community had not engaged in such activities, or had done so on a much more limited basis.

34 Tassos Papadopoulos, who was Minister of Labour at the time, states that after the Turkish Cypriots withdrew from the Government he was appointed as acting-Minister of Agriculture. When he went to the Ministry he found that there was a safe in the wall, and that after following the correct legal procedures the safe was opened. Inside he said that he found the minutes of a meeting between the President of Turkey, the Turkish Chief of the General Staff, the Turkish Foreign Minister, Vice-President Kuchuk, and Mr. Denktash which outlined plans for the movement of the Turkish Cypriot population to the north of the island in the event of the outbreak of intercommunal fighting. Tassos Papadopoulos, interview with the author. What is not entirely clear, however, is the extent to which this plan was proactive or reactive. In other words, was the movement of the Turkish Cypriot population planned with the intention that the Turkish Cypriot community

the case of those Turkish Cypriots who wanted to divide the island, it cannot be overlooked that there were a large number of Turkish Cypriots who were actually against partition.

This raises one of the key debates surrounding the outbreak of conflict, namely the question of whether the Turkish Cypriots were forced out of the government, or whether they left voluntarily. Needless to say, the Greek Cypriots insist that the Turkish Cypriots withdrew from their government posts was entirely voluntary.[35] Alternatively, the Turkish Cypriots are adamant that they were forced out.[36] In reality, and is so often the case with such controversies, the real answer lies somewhere between the two poles of opinion.

There can be no doubt that many Turkish Cypriots deliberately withdrew from the government. Some did so out of support for the cause of *Taksim*. On the other hand, many were genuinely fearful about the prospect of being held up as traitors within the Turkish Cypriot community at large and thus avoided taking a stand in favour of continued co-habitation in order to avoid trouble or recriminations. However, others were less fearful of their own side. Even though there was a strong element in the Turkish Cypriot community that wished to see the two communities separated, many Turkish Cypriots still wanted to participate in a unified Cyprus and wanted to show that the young state could be made to work. Many of these, however, had no choice but to stay away from their offices and place of work out of fear that they would be attacked by Greek Cypriots.[37]

Whatever the reasons, the fact is that by this stage the central government of the Republic of Cyprus was effectively in the sole control of the Greek Cypriots. Naturally, this served the purposes of those within the Turkish Cypriot community who wanted partition. Although the Turkish Cypriots' chief delegate to London, Rauf Denktash, stated that the Turkish Cypriots were not necessarily aiming at partition, but instead wished to see a movement of peoples,[38] it was becoming ever clearer that there were strong separatist tendencies at play. Vice-President Kuchuk, in an interview with *Le Monde* on 10 January, went as far as to openly say that he wanted partition.[39] He repeated this position a few days later in his own newspaper, *Halkin Sesi*, and stated that it had now become impossible for the two communities to live together.[40]

One of the most disturbing pieces of evidence that the Turkish Cypriot leadership was actively seeking to cut ties with the Greek Cypriots came on 7 January when the Turkish Cypriots put on trial the Chief of the Gendarmerie and the Deputy Commander of the Police Force, who were among the last Turkish Cypriots to leave the Greek Cypriot areas of Nicosia. At the opening of the trial before a 'Turkish Special Court' the two men were

---

would create the necessary reason for such a plan to be implemented, or was it created as a contingency measure in the event that the Greek Cypriots launched an attack?

35 Vassos Lyssarides, interview with the author.

36 Rauf R. Denktash and Osman Orek, interviews with the author.

37 Ozdemir Ozgur, interview with the author.

38 *The New York Times*, 7 January 1964

39 *Le Monde*, 10 January 1964. A supplementary comment in which Kuchuk stated that he had no confidence in the United Nations was later denied. *Cyprus Mail*, 13 January 1964. *The Times* had also noted that Kuchuk had stated that partition remained the best solution. *The Times*, 6 January 1964.

40 *Halkin Sesi*, 16 January 1964

charged with failing to obey the orders of the Turkish Cypriot leadership to establish an independent Turkish Cypriot police force.[41] Although both were eventually acquitted,[42] perhaps on the grounds of political expediency to show a united Turkish Cypriot position, the fact that they were even prosecuted highlighted that there were still a number of Turkish Cypriots who were committed to the existence of a bi-communal Republic of Cyprus.[43] Indeed, even at this point the main locations of the fighting were still around Nicosia and Larnaca and in a number of other areas, most notably around Famagusta and Limassol, there were still numerous examples of Turkish Cypriots and Greek Cypriots trading with one another and even continuing to work in the same offices. In Famagusta, where the district officer was Turkish Cypriot, even Turkish Cypriot civil servants were still turning up for work.[44]

Preparing for the London Conference

With the physical separation of the communities becoming more entrenched the Greek Cypriots started to prepare their position for the London Conference. As the Turkish Cypriots had feared, they decided to have two groups at the Conference: one representing the Government of Cyprus, and another for the Greek Cypriot community. The government delegation would be composed of Foreign Minister Kyprianou and the Attorney General, Criton Tornaritis. Glafkos Clerides, Tassos Papadopoulos, and Stella Soulioti (the Minister of Justice) were chosen to represent the Greek Cypriot community. The groups would also be accompanied by Paschalis Paschalides, the Government's economic advisor, and Sir Panayiotis Cacoyannis, an eminent lawyer from Limassol.[45]

Following their appointments, Makarios called together all the Greek Cypriot delegates at a meeting of the Council of Ministers.[46] During the discussions the Greek Cypriots proved to be divided between those who appeared willing to negotiate on the Constitution and those who felt that the Treaties of Alliance and Guarantee should be

41 *Cyprus Mail*, 8 January 1964

42 Osman Orek, interview with the author. In a letter of resignation written by Niazi to Vice-President Kuchuk on 10 January 1964, the Commander of the Gendarmerie had stated, 'Being aware that, instead of helping, I have harmed the heroic Turkish Cypriot community from my position and that from now on I shall not be able to be useful, I tender my resignation from the post of Gendarmerie Commander', taken from a Photostat reproduced in *Halkin Sesi*, 9 March 1964.

43 Christodoulos Veniamin, who personally knew Mr. Niazi, stated that the Gendarmerie commander was known to have been "happy and hopeful" about the creation of the Republic of Cyprus and had harboured a sincere desire to see it work. Christodoulos Veniamin, interview with the author. Incidentally, the commander had also been responsible for reading the appeal for calm issued by Makarios and Kuchuk at the very outset of the crisis.

44 In Limassol, for example, Greek and Turkish Cypriot dock workers at the port worked together for the entire period of this chapter. See reports in *Cyprus Mail*, 9 January 1964. This was confirmed by Christodoulos Veniamin, who was the District Officer of Limassol at the time, in an interview with the author. He also confirmed the story about Turkish Cypriots continuing to work in Famagusta.

45 *Cyprus Mail*, 10 January 1964

46 Clerides, *op. cit.*, (Volume 1), p.236

abrogated and the Turkish Cypriots given minority status.[47] Makarios was apparently committed to the more hard line point of view. However, he knew that this would never be agreed to in London. He therefore decided that preparations should be made to take the matter before the United Nations on the grounds that after the London Conference all efforts at peace-making would have failed.[48]

In Ankara, the Turkish Cabinet announced that Foreign Minister Erkin would head the Turkish delegation, which would also include Professor Suat Bilge, the Dean of Political Science at Ankara University, General Turgut Sunalp, Chairman of the Operational Directorate of the Armed Forces Chief of Staff and Ambassadors Birgi (NATO), Kuneralp (United Kingdom), and Eralp (Cyprus).[49] When the team arrived in London, on 11 January, Erkin immediately met with Sandys and Butler, the Foreign Secretary. Stressing the importance Turkey attached to the Greek-Turkish alliances, the Turkish Minister explained that any attempt by the Greek Government to side with Makarios would constitute a significant threat to that relationship. He then asked what the British position at the forthcoming talks would be. Sandys sidestepped the issue by saying that the British Government was not going to present a proposal at the beginning. When the same question was put back to him, Erkin was equally unwilling to reveal Turkey's strategy at the talks.[50]

With just a couple of days before the start of the conference the British Government assessed the positions of the various parties as follows:

> The attitude of the Turkish Cypriots. Dr. Kutchuk has called for partition. This however would be a drastic solution of the problem and, because of the distribution of the Turkish population over the whole of Cyprus, extremely difficult to implement.
>
> The attitude of the Turkish Government. The Turkish Government have all along been primarily concerned to secure the safety of the Turkish community in Cyprus. Their military build-up at Iskenderun was undoubtedly undertaken in order to save Turkish lives. M. Erkin said that new and better safeguards for the Turkish community must be worked out but the Turkish Government has so far avoided calling for partition or taking any formal attitude. They have also been careful to maintain the tripartite approach and they are undoubtedly fully alive to the dangers of any clash with Greece.
>
> The attitude of the Greek Cypriots. The Greek Cypriots have said that they want a conference to agree upon a unified administrative system for Cyprus which will be

---

47 *Ibid.*

48 *Ibid.*

49 *Cyprus Mail*, 8 January 1964

50 'Record of a meeting between the Secretary of State for Foreign Affairs, the Secretary of State for Commonwealth and Colonial Affairs and the Foreign Minister of Turkey at the Foreign Office at 11.30 a.m. on January 13, 1964', *FO 371/174745*

free from the possibility of outside interference. They have also said that if partition is suggested they will leave the conference.

The attitude of the Greek Government. The Greek Government are anxious to maintain their friendly relations with Turkey and have so far done their best to restrain the Greek Cypriots. But the present Greek Government is only a caretaker and will probably be unwilling and unable to take any final decisions. It may also be too weak to exert any effective pressure on the Greek Cypriots. It is always possible that the Cyprus issue will become an element in the Greek electoral campaign.

The attitude of Her Majesty's Government. Our principal objective is to arrive at a solution which will preserve our own good relations with the Turkish and Greek Governments as well as those between Turkey and Greece themselves. We do not at the moment wish to exclude any solution which will be satisfactory to all the other parties concerned.[51]

---

51 Briefing prepared for Professor Erhard's [West German Chancellor] visit, January 15-16, *FO 371/174746*

4

The London Conference

The London Conference officially opened at Marlborough House on 15 January 1964. As expected there were six parties present: the three Guarantor Powers – the United Kingdom, Greece, Turkey – the Republic of Cyprus, and the two Cypriot communities. On the first day each delegation was given the chance to explain its position. In his opening speech Duncan Sandys, the Commonwealth Secretary, stressed that the British Government, in consultation and in full co-operation with Greece and Turkey, had offered to help restore order and that this had been accepted by both of the island's communities. He also underlined the fact that the United Kingdom would not be able to act as a police force for the indefinite future, and that it was with a sense of urgency that an 'honourable and workable' solution to the political difficulties should be found.[1]

The next delegate to speak was Feridun Erkin, the Turkish foreign minister. Erkin emphasised the historical 'separateness' of the Greek and Turkish communities in Cyprus, and noted the strategic importance of Cyprus to Turkey as a 'continuation of the Anatolian Peninsula'.[2] He then offered a number of examples of speeches made by Greek Cypriot politicians that had indicated their total disregard for the Cypriot Constitution. Despite his tough language, he stopped short of calling for the outright partition of the island.

Following on, the Greek Foreign Minister, Christos Xanthopoulos-Palamas, took a much more moderate tone. After thanking the United Kingdom for its action in Cyprus, he explained that the situation on the island as one that had arisen from the complexities of the constitution, complexities that had led the Greek Cypriots to 'the point of seeing in their Turkish compatriots their opponents, their enemies.'[3] While he made it clear that the 1960 agreement certainly had flaws, Palamas was also careful to note that the situation had been made worse by the way in which the Cypriots had failed to try to apply the constitution.[4]

The Cypriot delegates then took the floor. Thanking the British Government for their, 'human interest in the tragedy of Cyprus as one of the Guaranteeing Powers', the Turkish Cypriot Representative, Rauf Denktash, followed Erkin's lead and avoided stating the case for complete partition. Instead he presented the argument for some form of federation. In his address he noted that the Turkish Cypriots were prepared to live with the 'Greeks', but

1 Written answer to the House of Commons, 16 January 1964. House of Commons, Official Report of Parliamentary Debates (*Hansard*), Period from 13th-24th January, 1964, p.48

2 Clerides, *Cyprus. My Deposition* (Volume 1), pp.243-257

3 *Ibid.*, pp.257-262

4 *Ibid.*

could no longer live amongst them. Instead, a solution should be reached which would allow the two communities to live side by side as good neighbours in accordance with the principle of a complete physical separation of the two communities.[5]

Glafkos Clerides, the representative of the Greek Cypriot community, rejected this view and instead called for the creation of a truly democratic constitution under which the equal rights of all citizens, regardless of race, religion or creed, would be matched by a government controlled by the will of the majority. Clerides made it clear that the Greek Cypriots would no longer live with a system that had created a complex system of checks and balances and which had been conferred on the two communities. This system, he argued, only served to make the smooth running of the state impossible and raised artificial barriers between the people of the island that necessarily brought about conflict.[6]

The final delegate to speak at the opening session was Foreign Minister Kyprianou, who addressed the meeting as the representative of the Government of the Republic of Cyprus. He presented a tough and uncompromising stance. He started by criticising the constitution and associated agreements as being unworkable and that they required changes. However, he rejected the idea that the two communities could not live together and called attention to the fact that there were 250 mixed villages on the island where no fighting had occurred and where the two communities wanted to continue to live in peace side-by-side in spite 'of some efforts by other quarters to move them forcibly.[7]

Turkish Cypriot delegates threaten to walk out

The next day, at the start of the committee session, the first major row of the conference erupted when the Turkish Cypriot delegation presented an official protest about the way in which the Greek Cypriots were attempting to represent the Government of Cyprus. Threatening to walk out of the meeting the Turkish Cypriot team declared that the Greek Cypriots must be recognised only as a community and not the Government of the Republic.[8] However, a crisis was averted by the quick action of British officials. Desperate to keep the Conference together at this early stage, they negotiated an agreement whereby the Greek Cypriots would have a community representation, but would also be able to have a separate delegation to represent the Government of the Republic. In return the Greek Cypriots accepted that the Turkish Cypriots could also be officially representation as part of the Government of the Republic of Cyprus, and that Osman Orek, the Minister of Defence, could be the Turkish Cypriot delegate.[9] Although this offer was never taken up by the Turkish Cypriots, the fact that the Greek Cypriots had accepted that the delegation

---

5 *Ibid.*, pp.262-273

6 *Ibid.*, pp.273-276

7 *Ibid.*, pp.276-278. In response to the question of the mixed villages, a Greek Cypriot spokesman stated that in fifty two villages 4,452 Turkish Cypriots had been forced to move by Turkish Cypriot extremists, but that in those same villages 5,548 Turkish Cypriots had chosen to remain despite such threats. *Cyprus Mail*, 18 January 1964.

8 Osman Orek, interview with the author.

9 Osman Orek, interview with the author.

representing Cyprus could not be made up only of Greek Cypriots was enough to persuade the Turkish Cypriots to drop their objections and let the Conference proceed.

Interestingly, this had not been the first time that this issue had threatened to disrupt the peace talks. Just before the conference got underway Orek had crept into the Conference chamber and had seen that there was a place for the Government of the Republic of Cyprus as well as for the two communities. He immediately warned Erkin that if this arrangement was accepted the Turkish Government and the Turkish Cypriots would be recognising the right of the Greek Cypriots to be regarded as the rulers of Cyprus. However, despite their strong intention to walk away from the conference, Erkin eventually persuaded the Turkish Cypriot delegation to stay and participate.[10]

In retrospect, the Turkish Cypriots have often regretted not having taken a firmer stand on the issue, either before or during the conference. At the very least they argue that they should have taken up their place in the main delegation representing the central government. Many Turkish Cypriots now see this failure to participate as having led to the conditions that led the international community to regard the Greek Cypriots as the Government of the Republic of Cyprus.[11] What makes the incident and its consequences even more difficult for the Turkish Cypriots is that this arrangement had been reached not only with the agreement of Turkey, but had been accepted as a result of direct pressure from the Turkish government.

A UN observer is appointed

At this point, the first direct involvement of the United Nations in the crisis occurred when General PS Gyani was appointed United Nations Observer for Cyprus. The idea of an was originally raised in public on 13 January, when it had been decided that an official UN representative was needed in Cyprus to report on developments on the ground. Accordingly, it was decided that the Observer would have full freedom of movement and communications but would not be able to receive any individual complaints on cease-fire violations.[12] Officially, the decision was reached following a suggestion from the British Government that had been accepted by both the Greek and Turkish Cypriots.[13] However, the process was not as straightforward as it may have appeared. Just a few weeks earlier London had rejected a request by U Thant, the Secretary-General of the United Nations, to have a representative present at the London Conference. While the official reason had been that Turkey would have opposed such a step,[14] in reality it was the United Kingdom that had feared the implications of having a direct United Nations involvement.

But even within Whitehall there were those who disagreed with the opposition to United Nations involvement. Sir Harold Caccia, the Permanent Secretary at the Foreign

10 *Ibid.*
11 Rauf R. Denktash, interview with the author.
12 *United Nations Security Council Document*, S/5514, 13 January 1964
13 *Cyprus Mail*, 8 January 1964
14 9 January 1964, *CAB 128/38*

Office, expressed his concern about the government's stand in a letter, dated 5 January, to Lord Carrington:

> The Secretary-General of the United Nations has already asked whether his representative should attend the London conference and we have said no. But I trust that this is not an irrevocable decision. I realize that certain kinds of United Nations involvement, particularly those for which Archbishop Makarios is working, may lead to a position where the Sovereign Base Areas are called into question. But if our attempts to resolve the crisis on the present basis fail, this may happen anyhow and the shape of United Nations involvement be less at our discretion than it is now.[15]

So what had altered London's view regarding the UN? The most likely explanation is the fact that by the start of the talks it had become apparent that the chances of finding a solution in London were very slim. This would naturally put the United Kingdom into the uncomfortable position highlighted just a week earlier by Sir Harold. In any case, on 16 January U Thant announced that his nominee for the position was Lieutenant-General P.S. Gyani of India, a former commander of the UN Emergency Force (UNEF) and the UN Yemen Observation Mission (UNYOM). In addition he also appointed José Rolz-Bennet, a Guatemalan serving as the Secretary-General's deputy Chef de Cabinet, as the Secretary-General's personal representative for Cyprus. Rolz-Bennet immediately flew to London to confer with the leaders of the various delegations. He then departed for Cyprus. During his thirty-six hour trip to the island he and General Gyani met with General Young and went on a tour of the Nicosia and its suburbs in order to view the situation at first hand.[16]

The conference reaches deadlock

While the appointment of both the Observer and the Special Representative was a welcome move, it did little to advance the hopes of reaching a political solution. In London the situation was proving to be as difficult as many had feared, but most had expected, prior to the start of the talks. During the committee sessions of the conference, which were held between the Cypriots without the presence of Greece and Turkey, the two sides continued to show the same intransigence as they had on the opening day of the conference.

In an attempt to overcome these problems, Sandys, Carrington, Devonshire and Sir Arthur Clark held separate meetings with the Greek and Turkish Cypriots over the course of the weekend, 18-19 January. However, even in these private sessions the two sides refused to yield on their original demands. At this stage the British Government presented

---

15 *FO 371/174745*. Having said this, the British Government did take pains formally to distribute a letter, on 9 January, to all 113 members of the United Nations in which it explained the facts about Cyprus and explain why it had become involved. *Cyprus Mail*, 10 January 1964. The letter can be found as *United Nations Security Council Document*, S/5508, 8 January 1964

16 *Cyprus Mail*, 20 January 1964

the parties with a document entitled 'Points for Further Discussion', which was made up of two alternative proposals. The first of these proposals was for the movement of the Turkish Cypriots into one or two large areas that would then be administered on the basis of a 'territorially divided Cyprus'.[17] The second proposal was for a limited voluntary population movement and the formation of local Greek and Turkish administrative arrangements. This would be in tandem with the continuation of the 70/30 arrangement at the national administrative and political level. The second proposal also suggested creating an international peacekeeping force with the participation of NATO countries.[18]

Both these arrangements were unacceptable to the Greek Cypriots. Instead they sent a draft memorandum on the future structure of a unitary Republic of Cyprus, a position that was, in turn, unacceptable to the Turkish Cypriots. Once again the United Kingdom tried to find some common ground and presented three further alternatives that were a synthesis of Greek Cypriot, Turkish Cypriot and British comments on the previous proposals.[19] This time the communal differences came out even more strongly. The Greek Cypriots held firm on their wish to see a unitary state. The Turkish Cypriots made clear their desire to see physical separation of Greek and Turkish Cypriots. The British for their part suggested, once again, the formation of a peace-keeping force, this time omitting the word 'NATO' from the text, and presented an administrative model that was a half way house between full integration as suggested by the Greek Cypriots and complete separation as demanded by the Turkish Cypriots. On 22 January the Greek Cypriots rejected these latest proposals. From that moment forwards the London conference existed in name only.[20]

Relations between Britain and the Greek Cypriots deteriorate

Despite their wish to see the matter moved to the United Nations, right up until the last moment the Greek Cypriots had tried to keep the United Kingdom fully engaged in the process. Two days before the final Greek Cypriot rejection of the British proposals, Kyprianou met once again with the Duke of Devonshire at the Commonwealth Relations Office. As before, he pushed for the idea of an Anglo-Cypriot bilateral treaty to replace the Treaty of Guarantee. He also pressed for the creation of a Commonwealth peacekeeping force.[21] However, the idea of a new treaty still remained unacceptable to London. Similarly, the plan for a Commonwealth force was also rejected. From then on a rift grew between the United Kingdom and the Greek Cypriots. Despite their previous close co-operation, no longer would the Greek Cypriots consult closely with the British Government and a marked change in the international politics of the Cyprus situation now took place.

The impact of the rift was also reflected on the ground in Cyprus. Because the United Kingdom had not come out on the side of the Greek Cypriots, anti-British feeling within the

17 Clerides, *op. cit.*, (Volume 1), p.291
18 *Ibid.*, pp.291-292
19 *Ibid.*, pp.291-300
20 *Ibid.*, p.314
21 *FO 371/174745*

certain parts of the Greek Cypriot community rose and a number of Greek Cypriot newspapers began openly to question the motives of the British Government at the Conference. One paper even went as far as to state that 'British partiality for the Turks is hardly concealed.'[22] But it was not just the Greek Cypriots who were turning against the British. On 21 January Turkish Cypriot police assaulted several members of the Truce Force as they attempted to escort two Greek Cypriot policemen to investigate a water leak in a village. Despite protests from the British troops, the two Greeks were then taken away to the local Turkish Cypriot police station.[23] Additionally, wider communal relations on the island were being affected by the fighting and it was reported that the Armenian community in Nicosia had become a target for Turkish Cypriot militias, which were alleged to be attempting to force them out of their traditional area.[24] Furthermore, in what amounted to one of the most serious, if only symbolic, attacks of all, the minaret of the historic Bairaktar Mosque in Nicosia was ripped off by several bomb blasts; an event that was criticised by both Makarios and Yiorgadjis.[25]

By now an all-out civil war appeared to be looming. Again reports emerged of a Turkish military mobilisation. The problem was that the United Kingdom's room for manoeuvre was now increasingly limited. As well as handling Cyprus, during the previous week London had been forced to respond urgently to a number of incidents in the East Africa – Tanganyika, Uganda, and Kenya – where local troops had mutinied against their British officers.[26] Given the deteriorating situation in Africa and Cyprus, as well as the ongoing troop requirements for Aden and Borneo, the need to replace the Joint Truce Force now became Britain's prime concern. Fortunately, just when the Greek Cypriots had finally rejected the United Kingdom's proposals at the London Conference and a viable British exit strategy seemed needed, the Greek Government offered a possible solution.

Greece suggest creating a force based on NATO members

On 22 January, Christos Xanthopoulos-Palamas, the Greek Foreign Minister, during a meeting with Sir Ralph Murray in Athens, suggested that should the London Conference show, 'signs of breaking down or of being very prolonged...He would put to [the Foreign Office] the idea of an allied police force to undertaking pacifying duties in Cyprus at considerably greater strength than the force which had hitherto provided.'[27] Palamas expanded on the idea as follows:

> [Palamas] explained that by allied he meant our own force with the addition of a substantial American contingent, possibly an Italian one and perhaps French. He

22 *Haravghi*, 18 January 1964. See also *Eleftheria* and *Ethniki*, 19 January 1964
23 *Cyprus Mail*, 22 January 1964
24 *Ibid.*, 23 January 1964
25 *Ibid.*
26 See *Keesing's Contemporary Archives*, March 21-28, 1964, p.19963
27 Athens to FO, No.114, 22 January 1964, *FO 371/174746*

> thought that if there was anything in this idea it should be negotiated in the capitals concerned rather than in the NATO Council...He envisaged a force strong enough to "impose" disarmament upon the irregular organisations of both sides in Cyprus and to bring about an elimination of auxiliary police...and eventually a reduction and so a withdrawal of Turkish and Greek contingents.[28]

The reaction of the Foreign Office to this news was extremely positive. As a telegram sent to the British Embassy in Washington explained, 'M. Palamas' idea of sending an "allied policing force" to Cyprus to keep the peace is very much in accordance with what our own first preference would be.'[29] When the options for peacekeeping had seemed closed, the Greek Foreign Minister's suggestion appeared to present a way forward.

The idea for some form of NATO involvement had first been examined by the British Government at the earliest stages of the crisis. However, joint action with Greece and Turkey was deemed preferable at that stage. In a telegram sent on 30 December to Sir Evelyn Shuckburgh, the British representative at NATO, the Foreign Office asked that Shuckburgh, 'emphasise to General Lemnitzer [Supreme Allied Commander in Europe (SACEUR)] that [the British Government] think the best means of restoring law and order lies in continuing the tripartite intervention undertaken by the three guaranteeing powers at the invitation of the Cyprus Government.'[30] The General, pleased with the Commonwealth Secretary's efforts agreed that the tripartite action 'should be left unmolested in their efforts to calm the situation down and subsequently to find a settlement.'[31]

However, on 7 January, another telegram was sent to the British representative at the NATO Council. After mentioning that, 'one obvious solution would be to propose the dispatch of a United Nations peacekeeping force. But there is a good deal to be said for avoiding this', the telegram asked for Sir Evelyn's opinions on the possibility of a NATO force being sent to Cyprus.[32] In his reply Sir Evelyn stated,

> It should in theory be possible for Her Majesty's Government to ask her NATO allies to relieve her of some of the military responsibilities in the Island or at least to supplement the forces under British command already engaged in maintaining law and order there...I am afraid, however, that I do not regard prospects in this respect to be very favourable. Our NATO allies would, as you say, be very reluctant to become involved in the dispute and still more to send forces to the Island. Moreover, I cannot at present see which NATO country could provide troops whose presence would contribute to pacification and which have the necessary aptitude and training for internal security duties. Certain nationalities (notably Mediterranean ones) would surely have to be ruled on political grounds.

28 *Ibid.*
29 FO to Washington, No.1058, 23 January 1964, *FO 371/174746*
30 Draft telegram from FO to UKDEL NATO Paris, No.2119, 30 December 1963, *FO 371/168982*
31 UKDEL NATO Paris to FO, No.505, 31 December 1963, *FO 371/168982*
32 FO to UKDEL NATO Paris, No.177, 7 January 1964. *FO 371/174745*

> Others (Scandinavian) would not be likely to agree. One is soon left with the Americans, Canadians and Germans. If we are to invite American help we might do better to do so direct and if Canadian, as a Commonwealth rather than a NATO country.[33]

At this point the British High Commission in Nicosia, which had been informed of the idea, sent a note explaining that although the idea of a NATO force would be popular with the Turkish Cypriots, 'the Greek Cypriots would plump for a United Nations and probably resent, if not resist, NATO intervention.'[34] In fact, this was exactly the reaction the idea received when it was first raised with Spyros Kyprianou, the Cypriot Foreign Minister, during a meeting in London, on 20 January, with the Duke of Devonshire:

> He [Kyprianou] was opposed to an international force being set up under a NATO umbrella. His reasons were that Greece and Turkey were both members of NATO; that he feared other members of NATO would leave "things to them" and that the result would be perpetuation of what he regarded as the undue influence of Turkey in Cypriot affairs. He did not [sic] consider that the pro-Communist leanings of some Greek Cypriots would be a major factor in rendering undesirable a NATO force. His own preference was for a Commonwealth force to undertake whatever peace-keeping duties were necessary.[35]

Options for a Commonwealth peacekeeping force

Given that a United Nations force was out of the question to the British Government, and that a NATO force was likely to be opposed to the Greek Cypriots, the idea of a Commonwealth force presented a third way forward. There had actually been several mentions made of the possibility of such an action in the previous weeks, either conducted by the Commonwealth as an organisation or by a number of Commonwealth member states acting together. Indeed, when the idea of tripartite action had first been put to the Greek Cypriots, Kyprianou and Makarios had remarked, 'that they would be far happier if one or two other unbiased Commonwealth countries were invited to assist.'[36]

However, and rather strangely, it appears as if the British Government never gave the idea any serious consideration. Quite apart from the fact that Britain might have been expected to take the work of the Commonwealth more seriously, especially at a time when British foreign policy was still conducted by two departments – the Foreign Office and the Commonwealth Relations Office – the reaction is also rather odd when one considers that throughout January Makarios had made many comments in favour of a Commonwealth

---

33 UKDEL NATO Paris to FO, No.16, 8 January 1964, *FO 371/174745*
34 Nicosia to CRO, No.110, 8 January 1964, *FO 371/174745*
35 'Note of a talk with Mr. Kyprianou on 20th January 1964', *FO 371/174745*
36 Nicosia to CRO, No.1066, 25 December 1963, *FO 371/168982*

force. Here was an alternative that Britain and the Greek Cypriots should have been able to agree on.

The eventual reason why London did not look into the idea became clear when Kyprianou met with the Duke of Devonshire on 20 January. The Duke finally explained that despite the apparent merits of the idea,

> [the British Government] preferred Australia and New Zealand to send troops to Malaysia rather than Cyprus whatever forces they could send abroad; among white Commonwealth countries therefore that left only Canada which was already engaged in a number of international peace-keeping roles and which might not be able to make a major contribution to Cyprus; India had her hands full with China and Pakistan was Muslim; that left only African Commonwealth countries as likely contributors on any significant scale and Mr. Kyprianou intimated that they would not be welcome. However he hoped that the Irish and the Swedes might be willing to help too.[37]

The argument against approaching Commonwealth countries, as presented by the Duke, certainly sounded convincing. However it is less than clear whether the United Kingdom actually made any attempt to sound out Commonwealth countries to find out whether they would be indeed be interested in participating in a force for Cyprus – either as a collection of individual Commonwealth members or, alternatively, as part of a single official Commonwealth peacekeeping action.

In any case, the idea for a Commonwealth force never received any real consideration. Instead the plan put forward by Palamas for a force consisting of individual NATO members, rather than a NATO force, was considered to be a far better proposal at a time when Britain needed to find a means by which to extricate itself from Cyprus. More a case of wishful thinking than a realistic option, the Greek suggestion for a NATO-based peacekeeping force was nonetheless seen by London as the only realistic way forward.

37 'Note of a talk with Mr. Kyprianou on 20th January 1964', *FO 371/174745*. On the subject of African troops, Vassos Lyssarides, although an opponent of peacekeeping stated that he could not recall such an objection from the Greek Cypriots. Moreover, in his view, African troops would have been preferable to British troops as they would have been more objective. Vassos Lyssarides, interview with the author.

5

Attempts to Create a NATO Force

Although Britain obviously favoured the Greek suggestion for some form of peacekeeping force based on NATO members, London was unsure about how the United States would react to the idea. Indeed, it was rather unclear what the US thought about the whole Cyprus situation. Throughout the first month of the crisis the United States had taken a remarkably low key approach, preferring to see the matter handled directly by the United Kingdom, which it acknowledged to be more influential given its historic position in the island and its constitutional role as a Guarantor Power. Although Washington was concerned about the impact of the events on the island on Greek-Turkish relations, it nonetheless disassociated itself from the Cyprus issue as far as possible.

This wish to avoid becoming entangled with the crisis was based on two factors. In the first instance, as explained by McGeorge Bundy, the US National Security Advisor, US officials 'did not want to put the Cyprus issue up to the president…because of the multitude of other problems that Johnson faced shortly after Kennedy's assassination'.[1] However, the United States was also fearful of giving the impression of any NATO interest in the crisis. This was highlighted prior to the start of the London Conference when a telegram from the British Ambassador in Washington stated that the idea of a British move to suggest that the United States might consider being involved as a participant in the London Conference would, in all likelihood, be met by a cool response by the US Administration. The United States wished to avoid an emphasis on the NATO interest and had actually suggested that a representative from a member state of the Commonwealth attend as an external participant, thereby avoiding an overt NATO interest.[2] More importantly, the same attitude had been expressed when the United Kingdom was first considering the idea of a NATO force.[3] The general spirit of US thinking on Cyprus was neatly captured by the US Secretary of State, Dean Rusk, who stated,

> We [the United States] feel that we should not inject ourselves into the substantive matters under discussion, but rather use our maximum influence to urge

1 Nicolet, *United States Policy Towards Cyprus, 1954-1974*, p.189
2 Washington to FO, No.4080, 28 December 1963, *FO 371/168983*
3 Telegram from the British Ambassador in Washington, Sir David Ormsby Gore, to the Foreign Office in London, 9 January 1964, *FO 371/174745*

> moderation upon the two communities and upon the governments most directly concerned without taking sides.[4]

However, with the support of Greece, London now believed that it could now get Washington to support a peacekeeping force made up of NATO members. In a telegram to the British Embassy in Washington the Foreign Office stated,

> Hitherto we had assumed that it would in fact prove impossible to persuade any NATO countries to contribute troops for a peace-keeping force...If there is any likelihood that they would in fact be prepared to give such an idea their active support we should like to pursue the possibility further...Please therefore ask the State Department urgently for their views on Mr. Palamas' suggestion.[5]

On 25 January, the British Ambassador in Washington, Sir David Ormsby Gore, officially asked the United States for its assistance in forming a peacekeeping force made up of contingents from NATO countries.[6]

The first response from Washington

The immediate US response to the suggestion from Ormsby Gore was negative. However, the British Ambassador was unwilling to give in so easily and turned up the pressure. As George Ball, the Undersecretary of State, wrote in his memoirs:

> [I] stated emphatically [to the British] that the United States did not want to become involved; we already had far too much on our plate...But the British were adamant. They would no longer carry the Cyprus burden alone, even though involving the United Nations risked giving the Communist countries leverage in that strategically placed island. The United Nations would dither and the Turks would not wait; tired of continued outrages against Turkish Cypriotes [sic], they would invade. Then we would have a full-scale war between two NATO allies in the eastern Mediterranean.[7]

Although it would have been tempting to view this threat to go to the United Nations as a bluff by the British Government, there is evidence that the United Kingdom was ready to follow the United Nations path if the United States declined to assist in the formulation of a peacekeeping force.[8] By this point Britain had a considerable number of troops engaged in

---

4 *Cyprus Mail*, 4 January 1964

5 FO to Washington, No.1058, 23 January 1964, *FO 371/174746*

6 Ball, *The Past Has Another Pattern*, p.340

7 *Ibid.*

8 In a Cabinet meeting held on 28 January 1964, the Commonwealth Secretary noted 'if it becomes impracticable to create a force drawn from member countries of NATO, it might become necessary to move

the operation in Cyprus, and, given the apparently open ended nature of the operation, could not continue to support peacekeeping alone. If the United States was unwilling to step in, despite the threat to NATO, then why should Britain? Although a move to the UN would obviously pose a danger that the issue of the Bases would be raised, this would have to be risked if the Washington declined to become involved.

The strategy worked. The British threat set alarm bells ringing in the State Department. Ball sought advice from his colleagues and met with the United States' Permanent Representative to the United Nations, Adlai Stevenson. Stevenson's reaction proved to be strongly in favour of US intervention in the crisis. As he said, 'the only way to deal with Makarios...was by "giving the old bastard absolute hell".'[9] Ball followed this with a meeting with the US Secretary of Defense, Robert McNamara, that same afternoon, 25 January. McNamara, although concerned about widening US responsibilities, was nonetheless aware of the seriousness of the situation in the Mediterranean.[10] On the basis of these two opinions, President Johnson that evening directed Ball to come up with, 'an acceptable solution.'[11] Although this did not amount to a firm agreement to go along with the British proposal, it undoubtedly showed that the United States was open to the idea of becoming involved.

The next day, 26 January, the British Government had another chance to outline its position to the US Administration when Prime Minister Douglas-Home, Sandys and Foreign Secretary Butler met with the visiting US Attorney General, Robert Kennedy, at Chequers.[12] At the meeting Sandys again outlined the initial British reasons for intervening in Cyprus, referring to the United Kingdom as the 'closest fire brigade available.' However, he explained that by this point the situation in Cyprus was such that a total of ten thousand troops would be needed to continue to preserve order and that as,

> Britain was not prepared to undertake this commitment alone, some form of international force would be necessary. No one was very keen on encouraging the United Nations to take too prominent a role and the most promising idea was perhaps not a NATO police force, but a force comprising contingents from individual NATO countries.[13]

---

to the United Nations to establish a military presence in the Island, in order to maintain law and order and to enforce the political solution, whatever it might prove to be. This course, however, was open to certain objections.' Cabinet Meeting, C.M. 7(64), 28 January 1964, *CAB 128/38*. In any case, the two options were by now being discussed in tandem. See, *inter alia*, 'Cyprus: Action should Conference Fail', 24 January 1964, *FO 371/174746* and 'Cyprus', *FO 371/174746*

9 Ball, *op. cit.*, p.341. See also UKMIS UN New York to FO, No.122, 25 January 1964, *PREM 11/4704*

10 Ball, *op. cit.*, p.341

11 *Ibid.*, p.341

12 'Record of a Conversation between the Prime Minister and the United States Attorney-General, Mr. Robert Kennedy, at Chequers at 2.30 P.M. on Sunday, January 26, 1964.' *PREM 11/4704*

13 *Ibid.*

At this point Sandys specifically mentioned the important role of the United States in the new plan and stated that, 'if the United States agreed, other NATO powers, Italy and the Federal Republic of Germany for example, will be prepared to play their part.' Kennedy asked a number of questions about the force, including how the British saw the situation developing in the long term and how long the force would be expected to remain in place. Without answering either of these questions directly, the Douglas-Home again restated the threat to NATO's organisational coherence, 'if violence got out of hand, the British troops had orders to return to the Southern [sic] Base area. When they withdrew there would undoubtedly be a war. Unless therefore we constituted something like an international force a war would be inevitable. As to the end result, no one could see with any certainty; but it looked as if partition would be the only answer.' The conversation ended with Kennedy promising, 'to take the matter up with the President on his return to Washington'.[14] However, Washington had apparently already considered the matter. The group therefore assembled again the next morning, this time in London. At the meeting the Foreign Secretary told Kennedy that, following a request from the State Department, the British Government was sending the Vice-Chief of the Imperial General Staff, Lieutenant-General Geoffrey Harding Baker, to Washington to discuss a number of questions relating to the structuring of an international police force.[15] Additionally, Douglas-Home noted that the Turkish Government was moving for de facto partition of the island, a move that would be wholeheartedly opposed by Makarios: 'since he wished to control the whole island.'[16]

The United States officially becomes involved in the crisis

Despite the contact between the Governments of the United Kingdom and the United States over the previous few days, in public the Johnson Administration had remained non-committal about becoming involved with Cyprus.[17] This position changed following a further Turkish threat, substantiated by another military build-up at the port city of Iskenderun, delivered by Prime Minister Inonu to US Ambassador Hare on 28 January. In reporting back to Washington, Hare stated: 'that the Turks were going to invade unless [given] some kind of answer [to the proposal] by the next morning'.[18] Washington now decided that the time had come to respond to the British request. President Johnson called a high-level meeting attended by Secretary of State Rusk, Secretary of Defense Robert McNamara, Undersecretaries of State George Ball and Averill Harriman as well as several Congressmen.[19] The next morning, 29 January, the British government was told that United

14 *Ibid.*

15 'Extract from a Conversation between the Prime Minister and the United States Attorney-General, Mr. Robert Kennedy, at 10 Downing Street, at 11.00 a.m. on Monday, January 27 1964.' *PREM 11/4704*. See also *The Times*, 28 December 1963

16 'Extract from a Conversation between the Prime Minister and the United States Attorney-General, Mr. Robert Kennedy at 10 Downing Street, at 11.00 a.m. on Monday, January 27 1964.' *PREM 11/4704.*

17 *The New York Times*, 28 January 1964.

18 Ball, *op. cit.*, p.341

19 *The New York Times*, 29 January 1964

States was interested in participating in the NATO force. However, two important provisions would have to be met. In the first instance the Cyprus Government must approve the force. Secondly, the three Guarantor Powers would have to suspend their rights of intervention for three months. Perhaps in order to give weight to this President Johnson sent General Lyman Lemnitzer, the NATO Supreme Allied Commander in Europe (SACEUR), to both Athens and Ankara to warn the governments of both countries of the danger that a Greco-Turkish split over the issue of Cyprus could have on the NATO alliance as a whole.[20]

The fact that the plan for a peacekeeping force made up of contingents from NATO countries had been approved behind the scenes led to rumours in the press that the Turkish Government was considering a withdrawal from the ailing London Conference. This speculation was confirmed when Foreign Minister Erkin arrived at the Foreign Office to see Butler and stated that the Turkish Government had indeed decided to withdraw from the conference.[21] However, once inside the minister somewhat strangely explained that contrary to the media reports no firm decision had yet been made by Prime Minister Inonu. However, Erkin did state that a decision would be taken on the basis of the conversation they were all about to have.[22] At this point Butler asked Erkin whether Turkey had accepted to join the proposed international force. Erkin said that his government would accept on the basis of two conditions of their own. First, the Turkish contingent of the force should be 2,000-2,500 and, likewise, the number of soldiers serving in the Greek contingent should also be raised. Secondly, the commander of the force should have executive powers to handle military matters. This was considered to be important as decision making was presently being, 'held up by the Cyprus Government [sic]'.[23] Butler replied that both proposals would be extremely difficult to meet. Erkin then attempted to introduce a third condition, 'namely that some indication should be given of the nature of the constitutional settlement before the force was created.'[24] Butler made it clear that this demand would be impossible to accept. Erkin then shifted the focus of the discussion to political matters and asked whether the British Government might prove to be sympathetic to the idea of a Cyprus federation. Butler stated that the United Kingdom had not discounted any idea as far as a solution to the continuing situation was concerned.

The minister left the meeting without offering any indication as to whether Turkey would continue to participate at the Conference. Instead, Erkin simply said that he had decided to stay in London a few days longer. However, the next day, 29 January, Turkey did in fact withdraw from the London Conference. Given the rejection of many of the demands made by the Turkish Foreign Minister during his meeting with Butler the previous

---

20 *Reuters*, 28 January 1964. See also Adams and Cotterill, *Cyprus Between East and West*, p.61

21 *Reuters*, 28 January 1963

22 FO to Ankara, No.475, 28 January 1964, *FO 371/174747.*

23 Telegram from FO to Ankara, No.475, 28 January 1964, *FO 371/174747.* The role of the commander-in-chief had in fact been a central item of discussion in Washington, see 'Commander-in-Chief of the Allied Force', in *FO 371/174747* and FO to Washington, No.1325, 27 January 1964, *FO 371/174747*

24 FO to Ankara, No.475, 28 January 1964, *FO 371/174747*

day, the move came as little surprise to the British Government.[25] The official reason for leaving was cited as being the lack of progress on the various constitutional problems.[26]

The Greek Cypriots oppose NATO involvement

At the same time as it presented the idea of a NATO peacekeeping force to the British Government, Foreign Minister Palamas also urged the Greek Cypriots to accept the suggestion and, 'warned the Cyprus delegation that Turkey was threatening to take unilateral military action and that it would do so even if we made a recourse to the Security Council'.[27] Moreover, the minister explained that if Turkey did invade then Greece would be unable to defend the island.[28]

Although the question of NATO peacekeeping had been discussed with the Greek Cypriots by the British Government, and rejected, the fact that Greece had proposed the idea obviously put the Cypriots in a difficult position. The problem for the Greek Cypriots was that they were opposed to the NATO peacekeeping option for precisely the same reason as Greece was in favour of it – because Turkey was militarily stronger than Greece. The Greek Cypriot case against NATO was explained by Glafkos Clerides, who was the President of the House of Representatives at the time,

> There was a school of thought and certainly there are still certain people who believe that the proposal for the establishment of a NATO peacekeeping force and its stationing in Cyprus should have been accepted. They believed that if Cyprus became a NATO country or, after the events of 1963, invited a NATO force into Cyprus, the objective of Enosis could have been realised and Turkey would have been prevented from intervening.
>
> This view is erroneous. If *Enosis* had been declared unilaterally, NATO would not have used its forces to prevent Turkey from landing forces in Cyprus. Its role would have been confined to preventing war between Greece and Turkey and by pressing Greece to offer Cypriot territory to Turkey. This would have led to partition. If, after the events of 1963, a NATO peacekeeping force had been stationed in Cyprus, non-aligned and Eastern Bloc support would have been reduced to a bare minimum. NATO interests in Turkey, which were always stronger than NATO interests in Greece, would have continued to be so.[29]

The Greek Government nonetheless pressed the Greek Cypriots to accept the plan. As Palamas noted, even if the Greek Cypriots were unwilling to agree at that moment they

25 *The New York Times*, 29 January 1964
26 *Cyprus Mail*, 30 January 1964
27 Clerides, *Cyprus. My Deposition* (Volume 1), pp.300-301
28 *Ibid.*, pp.314-315
29 *Ibid.*, p.323

should at least reconsider the idea as, 'an agenda for discussion.'[30] The Greek Cypriots refused, citing that there was no point discussing anything now that Turkey had declared partition to be the only solution and had left the conference.[31]

The collapse of the London Conference coupled with the publicly unconfirmed reports that Britain had approached the United States led to a backlash from large sections of the Greek Cypriot community. Already the media had taken to claiming that the United Kingdom had deliberately set out to deceive the Greek Cypriots.[32] As rumours about a NATO-based force spread, the Greek Cypriot press came out strongly against the idea. Editorials soon appeared claiming that a NATO force was simply a means to allow Turkey to intervene. Such was the degree of hostility to the idea that the negative comments persisted even after it was revealed that the ideas had originated from the Greek Government.[33] As the days went on the anti-NATO rhetoric was increasingly matched by calls for UN involvement.[34] At the same time statements started to be made in support of active Soviet involvement in the crisis to oppose NATO intervention. Interestingly, this was echoed across all sections of the political spectrum; AKEL and the pro-*Enosis* right wing were united.[35]

As must have been expected, Makarios refused to accept the proposal. Speaking at a news conference, on 30 January, the Archbishop insisted that if troops were to be sent to Cyprus they should come under the auspices of the UN:[36]

> The stationing of troops in Cyprus from Nato or any other countries with the object of preventing possible clashes between the island's Greeks and Turks is not necessary at all. I think that, on the contrary, the presence of Cyprus of these troops would complicate the situation and lead eventually to many adventures. Turkey can greatly contribute to the internal pacification of the island and the return to normality if she stops her threats of intervention, which constitute a constant encouragement to the Turkish Cypriots to resort to provocative acts and disturbances. If the presence of troops is required, these troops must be United Nations troops whose main object should be to repel outside intervention.[37]

---

30 *Ibid.*, p.305

31 *Ibid.*

32 *Makhi*, 28 January 1964. *Eleftheria*, 28 January 1964

33 *Haravghi*, 29 January 1964

34 'Only the UN can solve the problem' *Eleftheria*, 29 January 1964. 'UN over NATO' *Phileleftheros*, 29 January 1964. See the general Greek Cypriot press on 30 January 1964. In addition, 'NATO force a 'Trojan Horse' for Turkey' *Phileleftheros*, 31 January 1964, and *Eleftheria* spoke of a NATO 'conspiracy', *Eleftheria*, 31 January 1964.

35 The right-wing pro-*Enosis* newspaper *Makhi* stated that Turkey would face another Suez if it tried to invade Cyprus and that 'Russia will be better able to provide its support to Cyprus than it was in the case of Suez', *Makhi*, 29 January 1964.

36 *The New York Times*, 31 January 1964

37 *Cyprus Mail*, 31 January 1964

The Anglo-US peacekeeping plans are revealed

Even though Makarios had gone on record to oppose any proposal for a NATO force of any kind, Britain and the US finally revealed their plan on 31 January 1964. Under the proposal 10,000 troops would be drawn from various NATO countries and the force would be under unified British command, with central political authority coming from a committee based in London – a move designed to allay fears that the peacekeepers would be controlled by the NATO Council. Moreover, it was made clear that the proposed force was not actually a NATO force. Instead, it would be a peacekeeping force made up of contributions from those individual members of the North Atlantic Treaty Organisation that wished to participate.[38] The initial period of the force would be set at three months.[39]

It was also confirmed that while the force would include Greek and Turkish contingents, the size of these would be limited to 950 and 650 men respectively – the numbers permitted under the terms of the Treaty of Alliance. In Turkey, Foreign Minister Erkin expressed serious concerns over troop limitations for Greece and Turkey. However, following an all-night session of the Turkish Cabinet, the Turkish Government agreed to the proposal.[40] Similarly, following a cabinet meeting chaired by Prime Minister Paraskevopoulos and attended by military and political leaders,[41] Foreign Minister Palamas, who was still in London, announced that the Greek Government also accepted the plan.[42]

For the Cypriots, Foreign Minister Kyprianou automatically rejected the proposal.[43] He found popular support for his stand. Five of the main Cypriot labour organisations, including the Civil Service Association, denounced any NATO activity in Cyprus and insisted that Makarios' idea for UN involvement should be adopted.[44] Makarios, in spite of his earlier reaction, chose to avoid giving a response. Instead he released a statement noting

---

38 As stated by the British Foreign Secretary, Mr. R.A. Butler, in an oral answer to the House of Commons on 3 February 1964, House of Commons, Official Record of Parliamentary Debates (*Hansard*), Fifth Series-Volume 688, Period from 27 January-7 February 1964, p.815

39 *The New York Times*, 1 February 1964. A full reprint of these proposals can be found in James Stegenga, *The United Nations Force in Cyprus*, pp.41-42. From a survey of available British Government documents it does not seem to be the case that there were any important *un-stated* elements to this plan. Obviously the entire operational details would not have been known at this point, but it certainly appears to be the case, on the evidence available, that the US intended to be forthright in their intentions and not pursue some form of hidden agenda. Perhaps the most telling point as to how little the Americans regarded the seriousness of this threat, was the commissioning of a US Army Area Handbook for Cyprus. This handbook was put together in three months by one author (instead of the usual eighteen months by five or more contributors), this shows how sure the US Army was that they were about to take up peacekeeping duties. Thomas Adams, interview with the author. See also Adams, *US Army Area Handbook for Cyprus*.

40 *The New York Times*, 1 February 1964

41 *Ibid.*

42 *Reuters*, 1 February. It was also stated by the British Foreign Secretary, Mr. R.A. Butler, in an oral answer to the House of Commons on 3 February 1964, House of Commons, Official Record of Parliamentary Debates (*Hansard*), Fifth series-Volume 688, Period from 27 January-7 February 1964, p.815

43 *The New York Times*, 1 February 1964

44 *Cyprus Mail*, 1 February 1964. The other four organisations were: the Old Trade Unions, the Independent Trade Unions, the Democratic Trade Unions, and the Army Civil Service Union.

that he had yet to be officially presented with the terms of the proposal.[45] This was clearly a delaying tactic. The Archbishop had already made up his mind on the substantive points of the plan. This became clear at a cabinet meeting the next morning when he rejected the idea as being 'totally unacceptable'.[46]

Attempts to persuade Makarios to accept the Plan

Given that Makarios looked ready to officially reject the idea, Cyril Pickard, the acting British High Commissioner, went to visit the Archbishop to try to persuade him to accept the force. Although pressed to reply to the proposal, Makarios refused to give an answer. Stressing the Truce Force's inability to keep the peace adequately, and that a rejection would add to tensions, Pickard informed the Archbishop that,

> under no circumstances should any indication be given to the Press that the Government of Cyprus will reject the proposals now being mutually considered in London. The Government of Cyprus bears a heavy responsibility for the continued maintenance of peace in the island. Its responsibility is not only to the people of Cyprus themselves but also to Britain as the country providing the peacekeeping force.[47]

This did little to sway Makarios. Indeed, he again refused to give an answer to the proposals during a second meeting with Pickard that was also attended by the American Ambassador, Fraser Wilkins.[48] The Archbishop's silence became all the more frustrating after Vice-President Kuchuk announced that the Turkish Cypriot community had accepted the peacekeeping plan 'in principle', and that a firm reply would be given soon.[49]

Meanwhile the Greek Cypriot press took to attacking the British and US Governments for putting pressure on the government.[50] One newspaper even went as far as to invoke the spirit of the Suez Crisis and called upon the Soviet Union to come to the assistance of the Republic of Cyprus.[51] The next day a mass demonstration was held in Nicosia during which thousands of Greek Cypriot students carrying banners and chanting anti-NATO slogans marched past the US and Soviet Embassies.[52] Although Makarios himself later intervened to break up the group, the tensions over the controversial plan soon led to further fighting between the communities. A serious incident occurred when a number of Greek Cypriot

45 *Cyprus Mail*, 2 February 1964. This despite the fact that the *Cyprus Mail* had reported (with a front page photograph) that Pickard and Wilkins had visited Makarios, and that during the course of his two-hour meeting with them the plan had been presented. *Cyprus Mail*, 1 February 1964

46 *Cyprus Mail*, 2 February 1964. Clerides and Kyprianou attended the meeting, amongst others.

47 Clerides, *op. cit.*, (Volume 1), p.310

48 *Ibid.*

49 *Cyprus Mail*, 3 February 1964

50 *Eleftheria*, *Phileleftheros*, *Haravghi*, 2 February 1964

51 'We must ask Russia to guarantee our territorial integrity in the same way as Russia did for the UAR during the Anglo-French invasion.' *Ethniki*, 3 February 1964

52 *Cyprus Mail*, 4 February 1964

police crossed the Green-Line near the Paphos gate, to the east of the old town of Nicosia. Serious injuries were averted, however, when a Truce Force patrol went to the scene and managed to disarm the Greek Cypriots all the while trying to prevent the Turkish Cypriots from firing upon the Greeks as they retreated.[53]

By now the fallout from the NATO proposal was starting to take its toll on the Force. In what proved to be an unfortunately realistic appraisal, *The Times* stated that following the Paphos Gate incident, 'concern was being expressed in Nicosia tonight that the growing tension may lead to incidents involving the British Truce Force.'[54] Indeed, the next day, editorials in the Greek Cypriot press stated that the United Kingdom had 'collaborated' with the Turkish Cypriots.[55]

London and Washington were also becoming concerned at the degree of popular support for Soviet involvement in the island. Their particular concerns centred around the possibility that even if he did not invite the Soviet Union to take a direct stand on the issue, the Archbishop might be tempted to try to take the matter before the United Nations, where he would be able to get diplomatic support from the USSR. The State Department therefore informed the Foreign Office that they had developed a six-point warning to present to the Archbishop to dissuade him from following the recourse to the United Nations. The threats, and that is not too contentious a word in this case, were as follows:

> (a) If the Archbishop goes to the United Nations the United States Government will take the position that the question is not one of a threat to the territorial integrity and political independence of Cyprus but of a dispute between two groups within the state.
> (b) The United States will insist that both parties to the dispute should be heard by the Security Council (Mr. Eilts [the US State Department official who communicated the message] said that Mr. Rossides could therefore expect company!).
> (c) In any debate the United States will place the full blame for the situation on Archbishop Makarios personally and contrast his attitude with the constructive attitude shown by Dr. Kutchuk.
> (d) The United States will ask the Security Council to instruct the Secretary-General to mediate the dispute and will express the hope that he will choose a European mediator.
> (e) The United States will oppose any United Nations peacekeeping operation. They will do this on the grounds that in the past it has fallen on them to finance by

53 *The Times*, 4 February 1964
54 *The Times*, 4 February 1964
55 *Cyprus Mail*, 4 February 1964. There were numerous allegations made to this effect. In an interview with a Greek Cypriot ex-militia fighter who had been involved with the events of the time, the author was told how the fighter had actually witnessed British troops assisting Turkish Cypriot militia in their attempts to forcibly move a Turkish Cypriot community from their mixed village into a Turkish Cypriot enclave. Rauf Denktash denied this allegation during an interview with the author.

> far the largest part of most U.N. operations of this sort and that the Russians have not so far paid for any.
> (f) If unrest develops in the island and the Turkish Government decide to intervene, the United States Government will take the line that they are perfectly within their rights under the Treaty of Guarantee.[56]

Soon afterwards, the State Department sent another telegram to London to let it know that point (d) had been dropped on the grounds Makarios would like to see that happen. Instead a new clause had been added:

> If the Cypriots and the Russians try to take the Cyprus question to the General Assembly the American Government does not think that they can get very far because of the liability of the Russians to lose their vote in the General Assembly under Article 19 by reason of their arrears in payment of financial contributions.[57]

This particularly strong approach was supported by the British Government, which felt that it would go a long to towards persuading Makarios to avoid the United Nations.[58]

Whether Makarios was given this warning is unclear.[59] In any case on the following day, 4 February, Makarios finally returned his answer. Accepted the plan in principle, he nonetheless maintained that there must be some form of overall UN Security Council responsibility for the force.[60] Although the answer appeared to be superficially positive, the insistence that there must be Security Council involvement was a major impediment.

Britain and the US moderate their approach

Meanwhile the situation in Cyprus was proving to be a source of concern for everybody. Popular hostility towards the United States reached a new high when two bombs exploded outside the US Embassy in Nicosia.[61] Makarios, immediately responded by calling the, 'the culprits are the worst enemies of Cyprus...they have betrayed their country.'[62] In London, Foreign Minister Kyprianou, in conversation with the Greek Ambassador, noted the degree

56 Document dated 3 February 1964, *FO 371/174747*

57 *Ibid.*

58 At the bottom of the document the Permanent Secretary, Sir Harold Caccia wrote 'This is the sort of stuff that Lord Palmerston would have rejoiced to use or to hear from an Ally. Perhaps the P.M. as well as Commonwealth Secretary should be told.' Butler in turn wrote 'Prime Minister, As Sir H. Caccia suggests you may find some comfort from this.' Beneath this comment Douglas-Home had written, 'Good Stuff'. Document dated 3 February 1964, *FO 371/174747*

59 In the document it was stated that Eilts had said that Ambassador Wilkins would not 'seek a special interview' with Makarios in order to tell him these points but that the United States might approach Kyprianou in London to convey the message, or that Rusk may give it to Rossides in New York. Document dated 3 February 1964, *FO 371/174747*

60 *The New York Times*, 5 February 1964

61 *Cyprus Mail*, 5 February 1964. The newspaper noted: 'Two bomb explosions last night damaged a side-entrance of the United States Embassy in Nicosia, an unprecedented attack on a foreign diplomatic mission.'

62 *Cyprus Mail*, 5 February 1964

to which the Greek Cypriot leadership was 'increasingly worrying about the increase of communist pressure, and the bomb incidents yesterday had clearly scared them.'[63] In addition the Minister noted that while, 'he was now rather more optimistic, he was depressed by the way in which pro-Communist and pro-Russian sentiments were now being used indiscriminately by all shades of Cypriot political opinion.'[64] At the same time, there were attempts in the more moderate sections of the Greek language media on the island to inculcate their compatriots with more rational thinking.[65]

Sensing that they needed to draw the Greek Cypriots back from Soviet involvement, Britain and the United States now told Makarios that they would agree to UN Security Council authorisation, but only on the condition that the composition and instructions of the force be decided on beforehand.[66] Perhaps sensing that the United Nations might soon be called upon to get involved, the UN Secretary-General, U Thant, at this point issued a statement thanking Britain for its peacekeeping efforts since the beginning of the crisis and noting that the 'British actions were fully in accordance with Article 33 of the U.N. Charter - dealing with peaceful settlement of disputes and were "very appropriate"'.[67] However, while he was in favour of some form of UN involvement, if that was what the parties concerned wanted, the Secretary-General made it clear that the United Nation could not afford to foot the bill for any proposed operation – even if UN involvement was only nominal.[68] The next day the Secretary-General held meetings (assisted by his advisor on Cyprus, Ralph Bunche) with British, American, French, and Soviet representatives during which, 'a lot of ground was covered.'[69]

Any optimism that may now have existed at the diplomatic level was, however, being tempered by renewed violence across Cyprus. Fighting was now being reported in Paphos, to the far west of the island, as well as in the village of Ayios Sozemenos, just south of Nicosia. Naturally, fears again grew of a Turkish intervention. The seriousness of the situation was confirmed when Greece informed London that it would have to respond accordingly if Turkey did in fact invade.[70]

---

63 Note written by J.O. Rennie, 5 February 1964, *FO 371/174747*

64 *Ibid.* Kyprianou could not, however, remember having had this conversation. Spyros Kyprianou, personal interview with the author. Vassos Lyssarides, during an interview with the author, noted the way in which Khrushchev's name elicited applause whenever it was used at political rallies at the time.

65 See *Makhi*, 4 February 1964

66 *The New York Times*, 6 February 1964. Indeed, this was a more than desirable turn of events as the NATO epithet was doing considerable harm, as Sir Evelyn Shuckburgh noted 'I hesitate to intervene from this post but I have been struck by the following combination of facts:- (a) Nobody wants a NATO force, and indeed the misleading but unavoidable NATO label is becoming an increasing handicap to the current proposal.' UKMIS NATO Paris to FO, No.85, 6 February 1964, *FO 371/174747*

67 *Reuters*, 7 February 1964

68 *The New York Times*, 7 February 1964. *The Economist*, 15 February 1964, p.581

69 *Reuters*, 8 February 1964

70 Athens to FO, No.220, 7 February 1964, *FO 371/174747*

A NATO-based force fails to attract support

Another problem facing Britain and the US was the lack of support for the peacekeeping plan from other important NATO members. In the initial plan, as put forward by Greece, the idea was to create a body made up of contingents from the United Kingdom, the United States, Italy and France. However it was proving difficult to enlist their help. From the outset the French had shown little interest in the proposals; even though the idea for a NATO-based force, as opposed to a NATO force, had originally been pushed precisely because it was felt to be more favourable to the French.[71] On 5 February, the French Government announced that it would not participate.[72] Explaining why it would not take part, Alain Peyrefitte, the French Information Minister, stated that France had no desire, 'to become involved in an operation based on the Zurich statute, in whose elaboration she did not participate, and which moreover does not seem to her to be capable of lasting forever.'[73] Likewise, West Germany showed little interest in the idea. A special meeting of the cabinet, that had included the Chief of the Bundeswehr,[74] adjourned without taking a final decision.[75] In a memorandum prepared on the issue the British Government appraised the situation:

> 1. The following Governments have agreed in principle to participate; Denmark, The Netherlands, and Belgium. The following have said that they will probably participate and have agreed to start military planning with the War Office through their attaché in London without commitment; Canada.
> 2. The following have agreed to start military planning with the War Office without commitment; Norway and Italy. The following have said that they cannot send troops; France, Portugal and Luxembourg.
> 3. This leaves only the Germans outstanding from the point of view of military planning.[76]

As efforts continued to attract support from across Europe, little did London realise that the plan for a NATO-based peacekeeping force was about to attract just the sort of attention everyone had hoped to avoid from the very first moment of the crisis.

---

71 UK DEL NATO Paris to FO, No.51, 24 January 1964, *FO 371/174746*

72 *The New York Times*, 6 February 1964

73 *Keesing's Contemporary Archives*, June 13-20 1964, p.20116

74 *The Times*, 4 February 1964

75 'The Germans would like to help over the peacekeeping force but do not want to engage German soldiers.' UKDEL NATO Paris to FO, No.85, 6 February 1964, *FO 371/174747*. In fact, it had been noted that the prominent West German newspaper *Frankfurter Allgemeine* had warned the Bundeswehr and Bonn to avoid police action in Cyprus. *The Times*, 4 February 1964

76 'The International Peacekeeping Force in Cyprus: Military Planning', *FO 371/174747*

6

Cold War Tensions

On 7 February, the Soviet Foreign Minister, Andrei Gromyko, summoned the ambassadors of the United Kingdom, the United States, France, Greece and Turkey to the Soviet Foreign Ministry and presented each of them with a letter from Chairman Khrushchev warning NATO not interfere in Cyprus and expressing complete support for both Makarios and the Greek Cypriots.[1] Furthermore, the note called for the involvement of the United Nations Security Council in any further attempts to address the matter of fighting on the island. Most worryingly, the text referred to the fact that the solution proposed represented a 'factual occupation' of the island by NATO and that, 'the area of the Eastern Mediterranean...[is] an area which is not so far removed from the Southern frontiers of the U.S.S.R., especially if account is taken of how the concept of distance has changed in our time.' Moscow had made it clear that it was now fully involved in the situation.

This letter certainly came as a surprise. Until this point, Moscow had seemed curiously detached from the events in Cyprus – even thought many Greek Cypriots had repeatedly called for direct Soviet involvement. Reviewing statements made by the Soviet Government during the first month of the crisis it appears that the Cyprus crisis was low on the agenda. The one sign that Moscow had even paid any attention to the issue was a statement made by the Soviet Ambassador in Nicosia telling the Greek Cypriots that a letter had been handed to the Turkish Ambassador in Moscow on 31 December in which the Soviet Government stated that it viewed the events in Cyprus as an internal development and would oppose any attempts at intervention.[2] However, this was not seen as being an especially strong reaction. In London, the letter was simply regarded as a standard response, and did not cause alarm. Indeed, the British view was that the Soviet Union was really not that interested with the events in Cyprus.[3]

---

1 House of Commons, Official Report of Parliamentary Debates (Hansard), Fifth Series-Volume 689, Comprising the Period 10th-21st February, 1964, (London: Her Majesty's Stationery Office) pp.108-111 (Written Answers). The text of the letter can be found in the appendices.

2 British Embassy covering letter to the official Turkish reply to the Soviet letter submitted to the Foreign Office, *FO 371/174747*. The Turkish reply amounted to a restatement of Turkish aims and rights with regard to the Turkish Cypriot minority in Cyprus. Letter to the Soviet embassy in Ankara, *FO 371/174747*

3 The relative unimportance attached to this message by the British Government can be seen from the fact that although the Prime Minister thought that a reply might be in order he was advised against doing so as, 'there is nothing surprising in the Soviet message; it is an entirely standard statement of the attitude which the Soviet Union can be expected to adopt in situations of this kind...There might be considerable disadvantage in giving the Soviet Union a pretext for opening a round of correspondence on an issue with which they are not really concerned...Since the Soviet attitude has so far been reasonably restrained we would be wiser to

This relaxed attitude seemed to be justified. After Ambassador Yermoshin's comments AKEL, the Greek Cypriot communist party, sent a telegram to Moscow in which it congratulated the Soviet Government for its, 'unreserved support towards the Government and people of Cyprus.'[4] Embarrassingly, Moscow replied that the statement from Ambassador Yermoshin was from the Soviet Union's Embassy in Nicosia and did not reflect the official policy of the Government of the Soviet Union.[5] The only other voice of support from the Soviet Union during the initial phase of the crisis was a statement released in Nicosia by the Soviet Afro-Asian Solidarity Committee, which, purporting to speak, '[i]n the name of millions of Soviet people', accused 'some NATO members' of armed intervention in the internal affairs of Cyprus.[6] In addition, it declared its solidarity with the, 'courageous and peace-loving people of Cyprus who are fighting selflessly for the abolition of unequal treaties and for complete independence.'[7] However, this hardly amounted to a statement of Soviet policy, let alone a promise to defend the island. Moreover, the Soviet Union actually seemed keen to avoid any allegations of direct involvement with Archbishop Makarios at this point. When Rauf Denktash,, the head of the Turkish Cypriot communal chamber alleged that Makarios and Yermoshin had met on 28 December to discuss the situation, the Soviet Embassy in Nicosia issued the following reply:

> The Embassy of the Soviet Union considers it imperative to state that the statement of Mr. Denktash constitutes a big slander and is the result of imagination from beginning to end...this provocative statement aims at taking away the attention of the public opinion from the real causes of the bloody facts in Cyprus.[8]

However, on 13 January, the same day as the British and Turkish foreign ministers, Butler and Erkin, met in London prior to the opening of the London Conference, Denktash again claimed that Makarios was working with the Soviet Union and stated that once the 'Turkish factor' had been removed from the island, there would be, 'a communist coup in Cyprus and it would be a communist base. That is why Cyprus is a Cuba in the Eastern

---

give them no opening which might encourage them to interfere.' *FO 371/174745*. The Prime Minister accepted this advice; letter dated 3 January 1964, *ibid.*

4 *The Cyprus Mail*, 3 January 1964

5 *Ibid.* Gromyko later stated that: 'From the *very* beginning the Soviet Union came out in defence of the inalienable rights of the state of Cyprus.' Gromyko, *Only for Peace*, p.130. On evidence, as we have seen, this statement was not entirely true. However, this may stand as a vindication of Foreign Minister Gromyko - and by default the Soviet Union - as he had in fact shown an interest from the earliest point in the crisis.

6 *The Cyprus Mail*, 15 January 1964

7 *Ibid.* However, the Afro-Asian Solidarity Committee was not strictly an organ of the Soviet Government. It was in fact a non-governmental, anti-colonial wing of the Non-Aligned Movement that had affiliates in a number of countries, but seems to have been extremely close to Moscow – so close in fact as to raise serious doubts about is place as part of the Non-Aligned Movement. In any case, the role of the Committee was not to present official Soviet foreign policy, but was instead a mechanism to send out feelers regarding possible foreign policy options. Any statement it made needed to be treated with caution. The role and structure of the organisation was explained by Vassos Lyssarides, a former Vice-President of the Afro-Asian Solidarity Committee, during an interview with the author.

8 *The Cyprus Mail*, 19 January 1964

Mediterranean.' Indeed, he even accused Makarios of having Communists backing for his proposal to amend the constitution.[9] Moreover, Denktash had been noted as saying that Makarios deliberately worked to bring the Soviet Union into the Cyprus Crisis.

In actual fact, no clear Soviet role is apparent in the crisis until 29 January. On that day *TASS*, the official Soviet news agency, reported that the Government of the Soviet Union had said that the, 'tense situation that has lately developed around Cyprus is a matter of acute concern to the international public.' On the subject of the London Conference, the report stated,

> They [the Western Powers] are aiming at an encroachment on the freedom and independence of Cyprus...They are busy on a plan for some kind of an international force allegedly to protect Cypriots from Cypriots. The force is presented as an international one, but in reality it proves to be a force of the aggressive military-colonial Nato grouping...It is the major Nato Powers which intend to send the troops to Cyprus, primarily those who are already accustomed to using their troops against the national liberation movement of the peoples...It is claimed that these troops would bring order to Cyprus, protect Cyprus and Cypriots. Do they think in certain western capitals that people...become so obtuse as to believe that a force of this kind could serve such a purpose? Commonsense indicates that a State which for decades sought to subjugate Cyprus, to suppress its population, to maintain its military base there and hence to threaten the neighbouring Arab States is least suited for protecting the people of Cyprus...Certain participants in the London conference on Cyprus are aiming to bring the situation to the point of incandescence...to say that only machineguns, guns and aircraft are the means which can be used for ensuring order on Cyprus.[10]

That very same day a letter was addressed to the Secretary-General of the United Nations by Nikolai Fedorenko, the Soviet Union's Permanent Representative to the United Nations. In the note, U Thant was berated for having sent General Gyani to Cyprus as a UN observer. However, this telling-off had less to do with the Cyprus issue than with the Soviet Union's increasing concern about the overextension of the powers given to the UN Secretary-General. As the letter noted, 'It is the Security Council which, under the charter, is responsible for taking practical measures to maintain international peace and security.'[11]

Britain responds to the Khrushchev Letter

Despite the limited Soviet involvement at the earlier stages of the crisis, the letter from Khrushchev on 7 February changed the whole parameters of the Cyprus situation. As far as

9 *Reuters*, 13 January 1964
10 *Reuters*, 30 January 1964
11 'Letter dated 29 January 1964 from the representative of the Union of Soviet Socialist Republics to the Secretary-General', *United Nations Security Council Document*, S/5526

Britain was concerned, the note was not just an effort to embarrass the NATO alliance or to cause mischief. Instead London interpreted the letter as a clear show of the Soviet Union's political intention to force the question of peacekeeping into the Security Council, where, or so the British Government believed, they could exert influence over the island and perhaps hasten the removal of the Sovereign Bases.[12] At the same time Britain also believed that the Soviet Government's accusation against NATO posed a serious risk to the British soldiers serving as the Truce Force. Furious about the allegations, Prime Minister Douglas-Home issued a formal reply to the letter within twenty-four hours:

> Dear Mr. Chairman,
>
> I will not conceal from you that I have been surprised and disappointed to receive the message which you sent me on February 7 about the situation in Cyprus. I am surprised that the Soviet Government should have formed a view of this question which is so divorced from reality and I am disappointed that, on the basis of that view, you have seen fit to make charges which are as offensive as they are unfounded.
>
> Her Majesty's Government have one object in Cyprus. This is to help maintain peace and security of the island. This was why we acceded to the request of the Government of Cyprus for the help of British troops in maintaining order. This is why, in consultation with other governments whose interest in a peaceful solution of the island's problems is beyond question, we have been seeking agreement of all concerned on further measures to assist the Cypriots in the task of preserving their security. In all this there is no question, as you claim, of infringing the sovereignty, independence and freedom of a small state. I must say frankly, Mr. Chairman, that this is a matter on which the British Government and people consider that they know without prompting how they should conduct themselves in accordance with their Commonwealth traditions and in the spirit of the Charter of the United Nations.
>
> I sincerely hope that you will, on reconsideration, understand that the motives and actions of the British Government are not the motives and actions described in your message. I share entirely your view that the situation in Cyprus can only be made more difficult if passions are roused, especially when this is the result of external influences. This view has governed and will govern the policy of Her Majesty's Government.[13]

---

12 Moscow to FO, No.235, 7 February 1964, *FO 371/174747*

13 'Text of a letter from the Prime Minister, the Rt. Hon. Sir Alec Douglas-Home to Mr. N.S. Khrushchev, Chairman of the Council of Ministers of the USSR', 8 February 1964. Contained in the House of Commons, Official Report of Parliamentary Debates (*Hansard*), Fifth Series-Volume 689, Period from 10th-21st February, 1964, p.111 (Written Answers)

Other peacekeeping ideas are reconsidered

The fact that Douglas-Home replied so swiftly to the communication from Khrushchev did little to limit the damage caused by the letter. Although it was aimed at a NATO-based force, and was not a direct reference to the Truce Force, the letter nonetheless appeared to reduce the effectiveness of the Force. Soon afterwards an incident arose between the Force and local Greek Cypriot police in Larnaca after the police questioned the rights of the Force to conduct checks and searches.[14] This incident in turn led to Greek Cypriot criticisms of the political guidance that was been given to the Force.[15] The letter also gave ammunition to those who had opposed the British operation from the start. At a rally in Nicosia, Dr. Dervis, a leading opponent of Makarios', stated that the intention of Britain and the United States was, 'to invade Cyprus under the cover of NATO.'[16] In order to ensure the continued safety of its troops, London decided to reinforce its presence on the island by bringing troops in from Malta.[17] This in turn raised Greek Cypriot fears that the British Government was attempting to force a NATO force on the island by stealth. The situation was clearly spiralling out of control.

London now re-examined two earlier peacekeeping proposals that had both been rejected on a number of other occasions. The first was for some form of Commonwealth force. The second was Makarios' favoured idea of a United Nations force. Of the two ideas, London was certainly more in favour of Commonwealth involvement, even though it had been rejected several times in the previous month when brought up by Kyprianou. In a draft policy document on the subject it was stated that this idea could be acceptable as,

> Archbishop Makarios has himself all along said that he would welcome a Commonwealth force. One means of procedure might therefore be to say to him that, since he has refused the offer we have put, he must make his own arrangements to obtain the sort of force he wants. If this is to be from the Commonwealth it is up to him to make approaches to those countries from which he would wish to obtain troops. We would undertake to support his request in the Commonwealth capitals concerned and would offer to provide the commander and command structure for a Commonwealth force, on the understanding that a force sufficient for the requirements of peacekeeping could be produced. The Archbishop could either ask the Security Council to take note by consensus of its formation or alternatively he could ask the Security Council to pass a resolution approving its despatch to Cyprus. Although the Americans have been opposed to this idea in respect to the allied force, we would have no particular objection to it ourselves. Insofar as it could possibly be argued that the effect of such a resolution

14 *Cyprus Mail*, 8 February 1964
15 *Eleftheria*, 9 February 1964
16 *Cyprus Mail*, 10 February 1964
17 *The New York Times*, 9 February 1964

> would be to increase the degree of United Nations responsibility for the force, this would seem a good thing.
>
> The principal difficulty with this solution is the likelihood that it will in fact prove impossible to assemble a sufficiently large or sufficiently varied Commonwealth force (on the latter point it would seem desirable that there should be a minimum of three other participating countries in addition to ourselves).[18]

Regarding possible contributors to such a force, Canada looked to be a strong contender as it had already agreed to participate in the NATO force. Beyond that, it was unclear which other countries would want to participate. Another question was which countries could participate given the Greek Cypriots' desire to avoid Muslim or African forces.[19]

Therefore the United Nations option was reconsidered. The biggest problem facing this idea was the question of funding. U Thant had made it clear that the UN itself would be unable to foot the bill. Moreover, it was felt that the United States would probably hold true to its earlier threat and refuse to pay the costs of the force. Therefore, it appeared likely that the financial burden would fall upon Britain, Greece, Turkey and Cyprus.[20] The next problem concerned the structure of the force. If the matter were to be put before the United Nations then the Secretary-General would most likely take the lead hand in defining the shape of the operation. This would mean that the he would, as was standard practice, specifically refuse to rule out particular countries from the start. On the more positive side, this would mean that Eastern European countries, or countries in the Afro-Asian bloc, would probably be prevented from participating by the Greek Cypriots. The final problem was that Britain would also be excluded from participating. According to the precedent set by Secretary-General Dag Hammarskjold during the Suez Crisis permanent members of the Security Council did not take part in peacekeeping operation – and neither did states with a direct interest in the problem.[21] For these reasons London believed that,

> It would therefore seem to be in our own interests to go for a Commonwealth force...should this prove impossible to produce, however, it would seem preferable to accept a United Nations force rather than continue to bear the whole burden of peacekeeping on our own.[22]

---

18 'Cyprus: Action should Archbishop Makarios not accept the revised Four-Power proposal', 8 February 1964, *FO 371/174747*

19 'Note of a talk with Mr. Kyprianou on 20th January 1964', *FO 371/174745*

20 'Cyprus: Action should Archbishop Makarios not accept the revised Four-Power proposal', 8 February 1964, *FO 371/174747*

21 *Ibid.*

22 *Ibid.*

However, any decision would not fall to Britain alone. Turkey would also have to accept it. Fortunately, Turkey did not seem wedded to the idea of a NATO-based operation. Instead it would consider any option that would accept its participation.[23]

Meanwhile, the Greek Cypriots were still unsure about the situation. Although steps were being taken towards some form of UN force, it was shaping up to be a very different type of force than the Greek Cypriots may have originally expected. While a revised arrangement put to them omitted the term NATO, it only mentioned seeking a 'consensus of approval' from the Security Council.[24] Additionally, five NATO members had already volunteered to send forces as part of a UN force – Canada, Belgium, Denmark, the Netherlands and Norway.[25] Under these circumstances it increasingly looked as though a United Nations force would amount to little more than a NATO-based force by another name. In an about turn, the Archbishop now suggested that the previously rejected idea of creating a Commonwealth force be investigated further.

The United States takes the diplomatic lead

Although the British Government was now increasingly in favour of creating a peacekeeping force under the Commonwealth or the United Nations as a means to extricate itself from Cyprus, Washington remained intent on pursuing the NATO-based peacekeeping option.[26] With London obviously wavering, Washington decided to take direct responsibility for persuading Makarios to agree to its proposal. President Johnson therefore decided to send Undersecretary George Ball to the eastern Mediterranean to gain approval for the NATO-based force. This sudden determination by the United States was such that *The Economist* commented that, 'not much is now seen of the initial American irritation that the British should have needed American help at all. What remains is an air of harassment.'[27] This 'air of harassment' was no doubt exacerbated by the fact that Sandys even declined to join Ball on his mission, which Ball later put down to London's wish to

---

23 *The New York Times*, 10 February 1964. However, if the comments of Ambassador Kuneralp (Turkish Ambassador to United Kingdom) are correct, it appears as if Turkey may have accepted some form United Nations involvement three weeks prior to this. See comments in a memorandum dated 22 January 1964 in *FO 371/174746*

24 *The Economist*, 15 February 1964, p.580

25 *The New York Times*, 12 February 1964. The Governments of Denmark, the Netherlands and Belgium had stated their agreement in principle to become involved by 9 February. As had Canada which had agreed to begin planning with War Office through their Military Attaché in London. In addition Norway and Italy had agreed to start military planning without commitment, and France, Portugal, and Luxembourg had said that they could not participate. See 'The International Peacekeeping Force in Cyprus: Military Planning', 9 February 1964, *FO 371/174747*. The Dutch Foreign Minister, Dr. Joseph Luns, on a visit to London in late February 1964, at which he had a meeting with Butler, stated that the Dutch Government had agreed with the Anglo-US plan for a force made up of NATO troops for Cyprus. Indeed, it had accepted to send between 700-800 men. *Cyprus Mail*, 28 February 1964. However, on the issue of a United Nations force Luns stated that 'we are reserving judgement until we see what is going to happen at the UN. It is not certain the Dutch will take part in any force sent by them', *Cyprus Mail*, 28 February 1964

26 'Cyprus: Action should Archbishop Makarios not accept the revised Four-Power proposal', 8 February 1964, *FO 371/174747*

27 *The Economist*, 15 February 1964, p.591

limit its responsibility.[28] What Ball did not know was that by that point the British Government had all but given up on its efforts to try to form a peacekeeping force outside of the United Nations. As he left for the Mediterranean, the British Foreign Secretary, RA Butler, flew to New York to meet with U Thant and plan the next steps if Makarios continued to refuse to accept a NATO-based peacekeeping force.[29]

George Ball goes to Cyprus

On 11 February, Ball went to Ankara and Athens for meetings with the Greek and Turkish Prime Ministers. Although the Turkish Government said that they still favoured the Anglo-American plan he was concerned that Greece had by now made it clear that it would not accept any proposals that did not meet with prior approval from Makarios.[30] The next stop on his trip was Nicosia. When he arrived the situation was extremely tense. Over the previous three days there had been a heavy fighting in the large coastal city of Limassol as Turkish Cypriot irregulars attempted to establish fortified positions around the Turkish quarter of the town. The fighting had eventually stopped after members of the Truce Force arranged a meeting between the District Officer and the local Turkish Cypriot leader, which resulted in a ceasefire.[31]

In the early afternoon of 13 February, just prior to his meeting with the Archbishop, Ball contacted Secretary of State Rusk back in the United States to discuss the course of action to be taken with Makarios and noted that the situation on the island was rapidly 'deteriorating' following the collapse of the Limassol truce.[32] In Ball's view it was necessary to take a 'very tough line' with Makarios.[33] Rusk agreed and noted that it now appeared as if the Archbishop had 'delivered himself into the hands of local gangsters and that even a large force might be insufficient to restore order so long as Government does not want to maintain its responsibilities.'[34] Ball responded that, 'the real difficulty of course is that he does not want an international force and his bloody minded colleagues would much prefer to leave situation as it is so that they can conduct their murderous activities with impunity. However, I shall hit him hard on this this afternoon.'[35]

During his two meetings with Makarios, both of which were also attended by Pickard, the Undersecretary held true to his word and took uncompromising stance. As he notes in his memoirs:

---

28 Ball, *The Past Has Another Pattern*, p.343

29 *Cyprus Mail*, 12 February 1964. *The New York Times*, 12 February 1964

30 Ball, *op. cit.*, p.343

31 Christodoulos Veniamin, personal interview with the author.

32 Mr. Veniamin, during an interview with the author, noted that the cease-fire agreement collapsed after a decision was taken in Nicosia that certain Turkish Cypriot positions were to be retaken.

33 'Following is a report of a Telecon conversation between Mr. Rusk and Under-Ball at about 6 a.m., Washington time, 13 February', *FO 371/174747*

34 *Ibid.*

35 *Ibid.*

> [I described] in lurid detail the consequences if he [Makarios] persisted in his cruel and reckless conduct. The Turks, I said, would inevitably invade, and neither the United States nor any other Western power would raise a finger to stop them. Though Makarios tried to conceal his discomfiture, I had the odd feeling as we left the room that, as I reported to the President, "even his beard seemed pale".[36]

In a report sent back to London, Ball notes that he had called on Makarios as a man of God as well as a head of state to accept the plan, however,

> ...at the conclusion of my speech he said sadly and emotionally that he has to go to the SC [Security Council] because of commitments that had been made. Otherwise, he made clear, his government would be not only out but dead -- in fact, he said later in the presence of certain of his ministers, that, if he does not go to the Security Council, "some of those present in this room will not have their heads on their shoulders." Nobody smiled.[37]

Makarios had evidently made up his mind to go to the Security Council. However, the Ball kept on with his efforts to reach a compromise and rapidly improvised another set of proposals for a peacekeeping force, which he immediately put to the Archbishop. In a report to London he explained them as follows:

> 1. The GOC [Government of Cyprus] would hold up going to the SC until the latter part of next week.
> 2. Meanwhile the US, and hopefully the UK would put their full energies to the establishment of a force drawn from the UK, India, Australia, New Zealand, Ireland -- and, "if necessary", Sweden.
> 3. The Greek and Turkish contingents would not be included in this force, but they would remain on the island.
> 4. The terms of reference of the force would be to "assist the Cypriot Government in restoring law and order and normal conditions". We shall insist dropping out the words "the Cypriot Government." [This indicates that the United States had obviously chosen to recognise the Greek Cypriots as the legitimate Government of Cyprus by this stage.]
> 5. We had long hassle on the mechanics for guidance. The best proposal I could evolve with him was that guidance would be under chairmanship of the representative of the UNSYG [United Nations Secretary-General] who is now on the island or of some other representative of the UNSYG who would be sent for this purpose.

---

36 Ball, *op. cit.*, p.345

37 'Following is a copy of a telegram from Mr. Ball in Nicosia (U.S. Embassy, Nicosia, telegram no. 736) received by the State Department in the early hours of February 13', *FO 371/174747*

> 6. We had a major argument on the last point. Makarios insisted that he be the chairman of the committee providing political guidance; otherwise he could not explain it to his people. Alternatively, he would accept his own Minister of Justice. I made it categorically clear that any plan was impossible if his government provided the chairmanship of the committee.[38]

Makarios now called in three senior members of his administration with legal training - Glafkos Clerides, Tassos Papadopoulos, and Spyros Kyprianou. Later that evening Ball was called back to the Presidential Palace, where he was presented with a series of counter-proposals that they had been drawn up after he left.[39] In the document the Greek Cypriots stated that they would first want go to the Security Council for a resolution, 'calling upon all states to refrain from any act of aggression or from the use of any threat of aggression against, or from any action which may tend to undermine, the territorial integrity and political independence of the Republic of Cyprus.'[40] Once this had been achieved a force formed according to the principles previously outlined by the Undersecretary would be put together. Ball, in an attempt to change their minds, called on them all to sleep on the various plans before meeting again the next morning to discuss them.[41]

However, it was now clear that the Ball mission had failed. Although the Archbishop's final answer was still pending, the United States now saw two further options: Ball could return to Ankara and Athens for further consultation or Sandys could call another conference in London to discuss the matter with the Greek and Turkish Governments.[42] President Johnson supported the latter option, as did Douglas-Home and Butler, who both agreed to support Sandys.[43] However, it seemed a long shot. The apparent hopelessness of the situation was summed-up in a message received from Ball in which he said that he would now visit Ankara, in order to prevent the Turks from invading, and not to try to sell them a new plan. Afterwards he would visit Athens, 'for reasons of politeness.'[44] Washington now accepted the inevitability of Greek Cypriot recourse to Security Council

---

38 *Ibid.*

39 'Record of a Teletype Conversation Between the Under-secretary of State, Mr. George Ball in Nicosia, and the Foreign Secretary and Mr. Rusk in Washington, D.C. at 12.30 p.m., Thursday, February 13, 1964.', in *FO 371/174747*. In the message, Ball notes that: 'the paper had obviously been drafted by his three young Ministers (unhappily all lawyers) of whom he is a prisoner. From time to time he glanced uneasily at them to see if they gave him the nod. It was clear that they are calling the tune and that he fears both for his job and his life.'

40 'The Views of the Government of the Republic of Cyprus', 13 February 1964, *FO 371/174747*

41 'Record of a Teletype Conversation Between the Under-Secretary of State, Mr. George Ball in Nicosia, and the Foreign Secretary and Mr. Rusk in Washington, D.C. at 12.30 p.m., Thursday, February 13, 1964', in *FO 371/174747*

42 'Note of a Telephone Conversation between the Secretary of State [Butler] and Mr. Sandys at 2.30 p.m., Thursday, February 13, 1964.' *FO 371/174747*

43 President Johnson, the Prime Minister, and the Foreign Secretary all met at the White House that day. See 'extract from the Record of a Conversation held at the White House on Thursday, February 13, 1964 at 11.00 a.m.' *FO 371/174747*

44 'Note of a Telephone Conversation between the Secretary of State Sandys, February 13, 1964.' *FO 371/174747*

and instead formed a strategy to, 'resist any resolution which undermined the Guarantor Powers or the Zurich-London Agreements. [They] did not mind a "waffly" resolution (e.g., a resolution calling for no aggression against Cyprus) since nobody would pay attention to it.'[45]

Tensions rise again

As expected, the following morning Makarios announced that he could not accept the new proposal.[46] In light of the domestic political situation within the Greek Cypriot community, he said that it was imperative that the matter be put before the United Nations.[47] Kuchuk immediately called for Turkish intervention. As Ball had suggested, there was good reason to suppose that Ankara would act on the call as it was reported that Turkey was again assembling its Navy at the port of Iskenderun.[48] Moreover, the tensions in Limassol that Ball had referred to in his telegrams flared up again after a ceasefire broke down in the early hours of the morning of 14 February. Worryingly, the Truce Force was unable to intervene to halt the hostilities as it was being prevented from occupying certain vital strategic points by Greek Cypriot militias. Deeply concerned about this turn of events, especially after the announcement that the Ball-Makarios meetings had now failed, the British High Commissioner, Cyril Pickard, sent a note to Makarios in which he openly blamed the Greek Cypriots for the continuing violence:

> I propose now to make certain recommendations to my Government as to its future course of action. Despite reiterated assurances by the President that the forces of the State would not fight even if provoked, and a specific assurance by the Minister of the Interior last night of a cease fire in Limassol, at 6 a.m. this morning the Government of Cyprus forces launched a heavy attack. So far 150 casualties have been reported. Although a cease fire is now precariously maintained, we cannot ensure peace unless we occupy certain posts, in particular the Turkish Community Centre, the Castle and the Keo factory, and have the right to patrol. These arrangements have been refused by the Cypriot authorities. This, taken together with the reluctance of the Government to agree to the necessary peacekeeping forces and its policies as now explained, leads me to the conclusion that despite all assurances it is the policy of the Government of Cyprus to attempt to suppress the Turkish population by armed force. This makes any attempt at peacekeeping quite impossible. Unless I now have categorical assurances to the contrary, and these assurances are translated into immediate and public action, I

45 *Ibid.*

46 *The Times*, 15 February 1964

47 Vassos Lyssarides, during an interview with the author, noted that Makarios had told Ball about his intention to move the issue to the Security Council in a way that seemed to indicate that he had no other option. He was not belligerent in his tone, instead it was said in a very matter of fact way.

48 *The New York Times*, 15 February 1964

> propose to make recommendations to my Government on the basis of this conclusion.[49]

New Truce Force commander appointed

The inability of the Truce Force to keep the peace in Limassol was a clear indication of the degree to which it had become a victim of continued press attacks.[50] Even before Limassol, the Force had needed to adopt a tougher approach towards peacekeeping in the face of growing Greek Cypriot hostility. For example, just three days earlier, in what amounted to one of the most serious incidents concerning the Truce Force, a British soldier had been forced to fire a number of warning shots over the heads of demonstrators. This was the first incident of its kind since the troops had first been deployed in December.[51] As everyone in London now understood, the continued viability of the Truce Force was now being thrown into doubt. If it were to regain the initiative it would have to be restructured. Despite Pickard's threat to withdraw British forces, London instead decided to return General Young to his duties in the base and appointed Major-General Michael Carver in his place.

Unlike General Young, who was generally liked by the Greek Cypriots,[52] Carver immediately aroused suspicions. At the heart of Greek Cypriot concerns was the fact that he arrived with the divisional headquarters of the 3rd Infantry Division, the principal operation army headquarters of the United Kingdom Strategic Reserve, which took the total number of men in Cyprus participating in the Truce Force to around 7,000.[53] And even though he was not due officially to replace General Young until the 19 February,[54] on his arrival Carver at once began to restructure the Force and created two intermediate headquarters between Carver's Divisional HG and the troops in the field carrying out operations. Cyprus was now divided into two areas: the Eastern and the Western Tactical Headquarters. According to defence commentators writing at the time, this change meant that British troops serving on the island would now be able to react more quickly to local disturbances.[55] To the Greek Cypriots his efforts were seen as an attempt to change the Force from an *ad hoc* humanitarian action into a fully functioning military force.[56]

---

49 Clerides, *Cyprus. My Deposition* (Volume 1), pp.320-321

50 *Ibid.* See also *The Economist*, 15 February 1964, p.580

51 *Reuters*, 11 February 1964

52 Christodoulos Veniamin, interview with the author. This was also confirmed by Tassos Papadopoulos, in an interview with the author, who also said that personally he both liked and got on well with General Young.

53 *Keesing's Contemporary Archives*, June 13-20 1964, p.20118. 'This expansion of operations in Cyprus placed Britain in a very tight position as regarded its overall worldwide position. As *The Times* noted, 'with the departure of the HQ [3rd Division], the UK Strategic Reserve is now, for all practical purposes, totally committed to operations outside the United Kingdom.' *The Times*, 14 February 1964

54 Carver, *Out of Step: Memoirs of a Field Marshal*, p.316

55 *The Times*, 17 February 1964

56 Christodoulos Veniamin, interview with the author, Nicosia. Tassos Papadopoulos, in an interview with the author, stated that while General Young was not in Cyprus to, "enforce a long-term policy", General Carver has, "a lot to answer for". The Turkish Cypriots, on the other hand preferred General Carver. Osman Orek, interview with the author.

The United Kingdom calls for UN involvement

Meanwhile, Ball was readying himself to make a final, last-ditch attempt to secure a peacekeeping force that was fully under the control of Britain and the United States. Under a new plan put to London, he suggested that Makarios and the Greek Cypriot Government be bypassed altogether. Instead, the Guarantor Powers would form a new tri-partite peacekeeping force in Cyprus. Explaining the operational mechanics of the proposal, he stated:

> All patrols would be organised on the pattern followed in Vienna during the four-power occupation after World War II - only this time, three, rather than four, men in a jeep - and all operations would be conducted together. The force would stay in Cyprus until an effective international force, within the framework of the United Nations, had not only been created but was actually on the Ground, or until a political settlement had "been reached and translated into a viable organic document."...If the British went along with my scheme, I had no doubt that Inonu would accept it.[57]

London was unmoved by the idea.[58] By now it had had enough of the increasingly hostile environment on the island and was desperate to find a way out.[59] Therefore, on 15 February 1964, in a move that caught everyone unawares, Sir Patrick Dean, Britain's permanent representative at the United Nations, addressed a letter to the President of the Security Council stating that,

> Security in the island of Cyprus has seriously deteriorated and tensions between the Greek and Turkish Cypriot communities have risen gravely. This deterioration culminated in a serious act of violence in the town of Limassol on 12 February 1964. In these grave circumstances, I have been instructed by my Government to request that an early meeting of the Security Council be called to consider this urgent matter and to take appropriate steps to ensure that the dangerous situation that now prevails can be resolved with a full regard to the rights and responsibilities of both the Cypriot communities, of the Government of Cyprus and of the Governments party to the Treaty of Guarantee.[60]

---

57 Ball, *op. cit.*, p.348

58 *Ibid.*, p.348

59 As General Carver noted:'[t]his reinforcement coincided with increasing signs of anti-British feeling, which was developing in the press and being shown not only by the local population, especially the Greek Cypriot irregulars, but also by the Regular police.' Carver, *op. cit.*, p.317

60 'Letter dated 15 February 1964 from the representative of the United Kingdom of Great Britain and Northern Ireland to the President of the Security Council', *United Nations Security Council Document,* S/5543

7

The Recourse to the United Nations

Even though Washington had been opposed to a recourse to the Security Council during the previous weeks, once the step was taken the United States expressed its full support for the move – if only because 'it had gone as far as [it] could to try to deflect a tribal conflict. Now [their] only available course was to work through the United Nations'.[1] Likewise the Greek Government supported the recourse, albeit with some annoyance that it had 'constantly been advised by her allies in recent weeks to persuade President Makarios to abandon the idea of resorting to the Security Council.'[2]

More importantly, the Turkish Government also accepted the decision. This was in large part due to the fact that the British initiative had pre-empted action by Makarios, who would have used a Security Council debate to point an accusatory finger at Turkey.[3] Significantly, Ankara also halted its latest preparations for a military intervention[4] although it made it clear that it retained the right to take action should heavy fighting reoccur.[5] In contrast to the positions adopted by all the other parties, the Turkish Cypriot leadership opposed the step on the grounds that it would weaken the power of the Guarantors to act. However, efforts to persuade the Turkish Government to see this had failed.[6]

In the meantime, U Thant issued a statement in which he specifically called on the United Kingdom, Greece and Turkey to avoid taking any action that could aggravate the situation on the island and highlighted the importance of maintaining wider peace in the Eastern Mediterranean while the matter was before the Security Council.[7]

---

1 Ball, *The Past Has Another Pattern*, p.348. It is worth noting that even after the British recourse to the Security Council Ball continued to try to put together another plan. See Nicolet, *United States Policy Towards Cyprus, 1954-1974*, pp.215-218.

2 *Reuters*, 16 February 1964

3 *Cyprus Mail*, 18 February 1964. *Reuters*, 17 February 1964

4 A news report at the time noted: 'Turkish Air Force jets are patrolling continuously over Iskenderun Bay and international waters nearby, according to press reports reaching here from Iskenderun today. The reports added that Turkish naval vessels were waiting in a state of readiness at Iskenderun port, which is about 100 miles from Cyprus. The only civilian ship in the port, the freighter Giresun, belonging to the Turkish Maritime Bank, official shipping company, was now under navy orders and had marines aboard, the reports said. All roads to Iskenderun were under army control and suspect cars were being searched. Large crowds of civilians were going to Iskenderun quay each morning and shouting to sailors: 'Take Cyprus we have no more patience left', the reports said.' *Reuters*, 17 February 1964

5 *The New York Times*, 16 February 1964

6 This failure was attributed to the weakness of the coalition government in Turkey at the time, which was easily pressured by the United States. Osman Orek, interview with the author.

7 'Telegrams dated 15 February 1964 from the Secretary-General to the President of Cyprus and to the Ministers for Foreign Affairs of Greece and Turkey', *United Nations Security Council Document*, S/5554, 15

Upon receiving the news of the British request for a meeting of the Security Council Foreign Minister Kyprianou, and Glafkos Clerides, the Speaker of the House of Representatives, flew to London to confer with Sandys and other British Government officials.[8] When asked about the Greek Cypriot reaction to the British application for a meeting, Clerides, somewhat stoically, noted that London had presumably wanted to put its view ahead of Nicosia's and that while the Greek Cypriots wanted to place the emphasis on the threat of external intervention, Britain's request focused on the internal situation and underlined the rights accorded to the Guarantor Powers.[9] While the Greek Cypriot leadership was undoubtedly pleased that the matter had been taken to the Security Council, and hence the moderate tone of Clerides' statement,[10] within the wider Greek Cypriot community there were references to British treachery. The general feeling was that the United Kingdom was attempting to out-manoeuvre the Greek Cypriots at the Security Council by taking the procedural advantage.[11] Responding to this, and in an attempt to beat London into the Council chamber, Ambassador Rossides applied for an emergency meeting of the Security Council on the basis that Turkey was on the verge of invading.[12]

Within hours the various representatives to the Security Council had been informed of the two requests. That same afternoon, Saturday 15 February, they all met in the room adjoining the Security Council chamber in closed session to consider both the British and Cypriot applications.[13] Opening the discussions, the President of the Council, Carlos Bernardes, the representative of Brazil, noted that Rossides had been to see him to ask for the Council to meet that same evening and asked for the views of the representatives present. Sir Patrick Dean, the British representative, suggested that it would be better if the Council met on the Monday in order to allow the assembled representatives from the other member countries to seek advice from their respective governments. His request was immediately supported by Liu Chieh, the Chinese Representative. However, the Soviet Representative, Nikolai Fedorenko immediately took the side of the Greek Cypriots and

February 1964. The replies from the Greek and Turkish Foreign Ministers can be found as S/5554. The reply from President Makarios can be found as S/5554/Add.1

8 *Cyprus Mail*, 16 February 1964

9 *Ibid.*

10 In an interview with the author, Spyros Kyprianou confirmed that the Greek Cypriot leadership were not annoyed at the British action, as they had wanted the issue moved to the United Nations Security Council. He also stated the belief that, in line with established thinking, the United Kingdom had rushed to the Security Council in order to have a leading role in the matter.

11 The term 'ugly plot' was applied by *Eleftheria* (16 February 1964) who commented that the Cyprus Government should never have involved either Britain or America in its attempts to ensure law and order. *Haravghi* (16 February 1964) saw the move as an attempt by Britain and the United States to ensure NATO control of the Cypriot people. *Phileleftheros* (16 February 1964) noted that the NATO threat now seemed to have abated, but that there was now a real chance that Britain was attempting an 'occupation' of Cyprus.

12 'Letter dated 15 February 1964 from the representative of Cyprus to the President of the Security Council'. *United Nations Security Council Document,* S/5545

13 The proceedings of a closed session of the Security Council are not usually open to scrutiny. Unlike the open sessions, public records of the meetings are not made available. This is particularly frustrating as much of the work of the Security Council is conducted in meetings held behind closed doors. However, in this case a record was kept by the British representative and can be found as 'Record of Private Meeting of the Security Council at about 5 p.m. on Saturday, February 15, 1964.' *FO 371/174748*

called for an emergency meeting, citing the fact that the previous discussion on Cyprus, held in December, had simply been adjourned. He therefore argued that the Council had a duty to resume discussions on the matter at 'any moment' requested by the Cypriot Representative.

When asked for his view, the French Representative, Roger Seydoux, noted that without having seen the letter from Rossides he could not make a decision, and therefore asked that Rossides be allowed to address the Council to present his case. The Council accepted the proposal and Rossides was called into the room and more or less repeated the statement he had made at the Security Council meeting in late-December about the threat of Turkish naval forces approaching the island. Summing up he said:

> On the last occasion it was only the timely action of the Security Council in bringing these Turkish intentions before the eyes of the world that had at the last minute deterred them from actual aggression. The Council should meet at once before it was too late. The world would never forgive it if it did not rise to its responsibility. Monday would be too late. If the council could not meet at once, then it should meet at latest that night in order to pass a resolution designed to prevent or deter aggression by Turkey.[14]

Once again Fedorenko called for an emergency meeting. However, Adlai Stevenson, the US Representative, noted that Rossides had not added anything new to what he had told the Council previously and that he therefore supported Dean's suggestion for a delay. By now this view was also accepted by Seydoux and by the representatives from the Ivory Coast, Morocco, and Norway. However, both the Bolivian and Czech Representatives took the Cypriot position. As the figure now stood at four in favour of an emergency meeting and six against, Bernardes called a meeting for Monday 17 February. However, he noted that he would remain closely in touch with events through the Secretary-General and would be prepared to call a meeting within an hour of so if necessary.[15] At this point, Fedorenko accused the Council of acting irresponsibly and repeated his view that Cyprus was entitled to bring the 'continuing' matter to the attention of the Security Council. However, his outburst had little effect. Similarly, the next day Rossides wrote another letter to the President of the Security Council again asking for an emergency meeting. Bernardes did not act on the note.

Planning for the debate

Meanwhile, in London, the Greek Cypriot delegates had finished their discussions with the British Government. Speaking to the press prior to his departure for New York, Foreign Minister Kyprianou noted that the Greek Cypriots were, 'in agreement with the British

14 *Ibid.*
15 *Ibid.*

Government that an early meeting of the Security Council is necessary.'[16] He did not say, however, whether the two parties had reached any agreement on the shape of the debate.

When they arrived in the United States, later that same day, they were immediately joined by Rossides and Tassos Papadopoulos, the Minister for Labour, who had been in New York for the previous month after leaving the London Conference.[17] Soon afterwards Dimitri Bitsios, the Greek Permanent Representative at the United Nations, called on them. In the private discussions that followed the Greek Cypriots, in contrast to their public statements, not only allegedly expressed their bitter feelings about both the British and Turkish positions, but also complained to Bitsios about the lack of support they had received from the Greek Government.[18] However, as Bitsios noted in his account of events, the Greek Cypriots were nonetheless nervous about forthcoming events at the United Nations, and asked him how he saw their chances in the Council.[19] In reply he raised a number of points about a possible Greek Cypriot draft resolution that might be presented to the Security Council. In particular, Bitsios explained that any draft prepared by the Greek Cypriots would have to be put to the Security Council through the representative of a friendly state. As far as the wording of a resolution was concerned, he specifically warned Clerides and Kyprianou about the danger inherent in the use of the word 'recognise' in respect of the Government of Cyprus, informing them that the term 'respect' immediately made the issue of recognition redundant and therefore unlikely to be a discussion point.[20]

While the Greek Cypriots formed their own strategy, albeit with the assistance of the Greek Representative, the Governments of the United Kingdom and the United States were busy planning their own course of action. Given its success in the gaining the procedural advantage, the British Government was in a fairly strong position. It had the outward support of the United States, which had by now declared that it would respect Makarios's

16 *Cyprus Mail*, 17 February 1964

17 Clerides notes that: 'Makarios had doubts whether Spyros Kyprianou, Tassos Papadopoulos and Rossides could work well together. He felt also that it would be difficult to tell Rossides to take a back seat and let the case be presented by Spyros Kyprianou. Rossides was an old member of the Ethnarchic Circle and Kyprianou a relative newcomer. Moreover Rossides had attended, before independence, many debates of the Cyprus problem at the U.N. and other international conferences.' Clerides, *Cyprus. My Deposition* (Volume 2), p.45. While Papadopoulos seemed to have certain problems with Rossides, he was nonetheless keen to point out that for all his faults Rossides was honourable in his intentions. Tassos Papadopoulos, interview with the author.

18 Bitsios,*Cyprus. The Vulnerable Republic*, p.138

19 *Ibid.* Despite his views on Rossides, Tassos Papadopoulos, like Clerides, notes that the Cypriot Representative at the United Nations was in fact considerably more experienced than Bitsios with the workings of the Organisation. Tassos Papadopoulos, interview with the author.

20 Bitsios, *op. cit.*, p.139 On the matter of Bitsios's assistance to the Greek Cypriots, Spyros Kyprianou noted that Bitsios had indeed been "very helpful". He also went on to say that the Greek Government had been on the whole supportive of the Greek Cypriots, "especially at the United Nations", Spyros Kyprianou, interview with the author. In contrast with this view Tassos Papadopoulos, the Minister of Labour at the time, who had been in New York and had worked with Bitsios, stated that in his view the Greek Representative had not always shown the "heart to look out for the best interests of Cyprus". Tassos Papadopoulos, interview with the author. The tone with which this was said perhaps suggests that there were those who saw the whole process - including the advice given by Bitsios - as being geared to establishing a quick-fix solution that would favour the United States, the United Kingdom and Turkey.

wishes and that it would not suggest that US troops participate in any peacekeeping force.[21] (It is perhaps worth noting that the pressures exerted on the Truce Force had by this point made British interest in participating in a future United Nations force less than certain.[22]) Given that London had also received an endorsement for its strategy from President Gursel of Turkey,[23] it was clear that the best tactic at this stage would be to try to isolate the Greek Cypriots as much as possible diplomatically and push a resolution through as fast as possible.

The first day of the debate

By Monday, the day of the debate, the two camps were clear about their respective strategies and overall objectives. That morning Clerides and Kyprianou met with U Thant, the UN Secretary-General. Also at the meeting were Jose Rolz Bennet, and Ralph Bunche, the UN Under-Secretary-General for Political Affairs (who eventually decided the acronym UNFICYP[24]), who explained the basic six provisions of a proposal being proposed by U Thant:[25]

> 1. A plan should be submitted to the Security Council by the Governments of Cyprus, Greece, Turkey, and the United Kingdom for approval by the Council. A plan should be envisioned which would give full weight to the primary responsibility of the Government of Cyprus and of the three other Governments principally concerned, while providing for an appropriate United Nations participation.
> 2. A force to be stationed in Cyprus for not more than three months would be established by agreement among the Governments concerned.
> 3. The purpose of the force would be to preserve international peace and security and to that end prevent intercommunal fighting.
> 4. The appointment of a mediator, designated by the Secretary-General, with the approval of the four Governments.
> 5. No costs arising out of the foregoing arrangements would be chargeable to the United Nations.

---

21 *The New York Times*, 16 February 1964

22 In a meeting of the British Cabinet, Duncan Sandys noted that, 'the function of maintaining law and order in the island was imposing an increasing strain on our troops, whose relationship with the Greek and Turkish communities were inevitable deteriorating. We must therefore seek to ensure that, if a new peace-keeping force were established under United Nations auspices, United Kingdom troops would not be called upon to play too prominent a part in it.' C.M. (12), 18 February 1964, *CAB 128/38*

23 *The New York Times*, 17 February 1964

24 'Bunche wrote a long list of possible acronyms for the Cyprus force, including UNFIC, UNCYMED, UNFINC, UNCYMFI, and UNFORIC.' Urquhart, *Ralph Bunche*, p.369n

25 Bitsios, *op. cit.*, p.140. Kyprianou noted that the Secretary General was extremely interested in what they had to say and that overall he was "very objective, and very honest". When asked about the relationship that the Greek Cypriots had with Rolz-Bennet and Bunche, he noted that they "had all got on very well indeed". Spyros Kyprianou, interview with the author.

> 6. The Security Council would by resolution endorse the foregoing arrangements, call upon all Member States to respect the independence and territorial integrity and unity of Cyprus, and appoint an advisory group of three of its Members to be consulted by the Secretary-General on matters pertinent to the resolution.[26]

However, in a telegram from Clerides to Makarios the same day, the Greek Cypriots noted that the Secretary-General's plan proved unsatisfactory on four counts, namely:

> (a.) The terms of reference are not adequate. It does not specifically state that the force is for the purpose of assisting the Government to restore law and order, which is very material, and to bring about conditions of normality.
> (b.) Although it gives a hint that the force will also be entrusted with the defence of the Republic from external attack, it does not make that object sufficiently clear.
> (c.) The provisions about a mediator to be appointed by the Secretary-General still leave out the terms of reference of the mediator.
> (d.) No direct reference is made to the question of the Treaties as forming part of the dispute.[27]

Despite the unsatisfactory nature of the plan on these counts, it was now becoming obvious to Clerides that at least some of these key points of issue would have to be negotiated if a resolution introducing a UN force was to be passed.

When the eleven members of the Security Council convened later that day, the session was immediately adjourned for twenty-four hours to allow the Secretary-General to seek further agreement from the United Kingdom, Greece, Turkey, and Cyprus on his proposals for a force. Clerides sent another memo to Makarios again outlining his thoughts on the proposals and laying out his views on how to proceed. Makarios replied by proposing that delineation be introduced between the matter of the recognition of Cyprus' territorial integrity and the issue of the introduction of a force.[28] Disagreeing with any move to separate the issues, Clerides pointed out that any attempt to distinguish on the matters without a full agreement of the overall issues would be doomed to fail as it would be opposed by the Western Powers. Makarios believed that this was nonetheless a risk worth taking.[29]

That afternoon George Ball, Adlai Stevenson and two undersecretaries at the State Department, Phillips Talbot and Harlan Cleveland, paid a visit to Bitsios.[30] It rapidly became apparent that the United States wanted the Greek representative to lean on the Greek Cypriots to approve a draft resolution that they had drawn up in conjunction with the United Kingdom, and which noted the central importance of the 1960 Treaties.

---

26 Clerides, *op. cit.*, (Volume 2), p.48
27 *Ibid.*, p.49
28 *Ibid.*, p.50
29 *Ibid.*
30 The events are recounted in Bitsios, *op. cit.*, p.143-146

Furthermore, the draft clearly reflected the Turkish position on the issue, referring to 'states and authorities', and arguing that the Republic of Cyprus lasted only as long as the Treaties were respected. Bitsios refused to show the proposed resolution to the Cypriots. The delegation, clearly frustrated, asked Bitsios for his advice on how best to deal with the Greek Cypriots. Bitsios told them that the proposal put forward by U Thant should be seriously considered.

Fighting increases in Cyprus

In Cyprus, the situation took another turn for the worse.[31] In the west of the island fighting renewed around the village of Polis, where five hundred Turkish Cypriots were under siege in a school after the Truce Force contingent in the village had withdrawn to help calm the fighting in Limassol a few days earlier.[32] Fortunately, the returning troops were able to arrange for a three-day cease-fire.[33] General Gyani, who was on hand to witness the situation, praised the Truce Force, saying that 'the British Officers were showing much tact in an extremely difficult task on the island.'[34]

By this point the combined number of fighters in both communities was estimated to be in the tens of thousands with a constant supply of weapons flowing in to the Greek Cypriot community from abroad[35] – mainly from communist East European countries.[36] This quickly led to more fighting as the newly replenished Greek Cypriots attempted to break the deadlock in a number of areas around the island. Needless to say, this put the Truce Force under even more pressure and a further reinforcement was ordered by London.[37] By now the British troops in Cyprus were working under extremely difficult conditions and were losing the last remaining trust of the Greek Cypriots. This was highlighted when, on 15 February, Greek Cypriot irregulars abducted three unarmed

---

31 Lord Carver in his memoirs gives only the briefest of accounts of the period of the Security Council debate leading to UN Resolution 186. In an account limited to one paragraph he characterises the period as being of 'comparative calm...disturbed by two abductions of Turks by Greeks, which involved me bringing pressure to bear on the leaders of both sides to prevent the incidents escalating and to obtain the release of the hostages, of whom both sides held a considerable number.' Carver, *Out of Step*, p.317. Given that the chapter in which he discusses his involvement in Cyprus in 1964 continues for another twenty-two pages one can immediately see that he, like a number of other commentators, has focussed on the period following Resolution 186.

32 *The Times*, 18 February 1964

33 However, the Greek Cypriots seemed to feel that the events in Polis had been dramatically over exaggerated, for example, '[a]n official Greek Cypriot spokesman yesterday charged Turkish Cypriot extremists with exploiting the situation at Polis and circulating unfounded and malicious rumours in a frantic effort to increase tension and cause, wherever possible, incidents as a means of countering the Government's move in the Security Council.' *Cyprus Mail*, 18 February 1964

34 *The Times*, 18 February 1964

35 *Ibid.* The Cyprus Government did not deny the fact that it had acquired arms stating that it had approached Britain on 31 December 1963 about possible arms purchases from the United Kingdom but had been refused. After this they therefore 'went to other [unspecified] sources.' *Reuters*, 17 February 1964.

36 Chris Economides, interview with the author.

37 *The Times*, 17 February 1964

military police dog handlers in a private car as they drove to Larnaca.[38] Although they were handed over unharmed to the British Army the next morning, following strong protests from Pickard and Air Chief Marshal Barnett, the overall commander of the Sovereign Base Areas, it was becoming obvious that the Truce Force was rapidly losing the last vestiges of its ability to keep the peace.[39]

The Security Council debate begins

With growing political differences between the Greek Cypriots and the United Kingdom in New York, and the situation in Cyprus deteriorating, the stage was now set for a showdown when, on the afternoon of 18 February 1964, the Security Council reconvened before a large audience. Despite an immediate Soviet demand that the opening statement be made by the Cyprus Government,[40] Bernardes instead gave the floor to Sir Patrick Dean.[41] Dean began by outlining the process leading to the independence of Cyprus and the Treaty of Guarantee. After explaining each article of the Treaty, he told the Council that the Basic Articles of the Constitution of Cyprus, of which the Treaty of Guarantee was a part, were not open to amendment 'by way of variation, addition or repeal. Their principal purpose is to ensure that the rights and interests of the two major communities, that is to say, the Greek Cypriots and the Turkish Cypriots, in the island shall be fully respected and kept in balance.'[42]

Dean then summarised the events leading to the British involvement in the island following the outbreak of fighting and explained the steps taken by the British Government since then, including the presentation of the two international plans for a peace-keeping force – omitting the word NATO altogether. The rejection of these had led to the decision

---

38 *Cyprus Mail*, 17 February 1964

39 *The Times*, 17 February 1964

40 In fact the Soviet Union Permanent Representative chose to give a long address on this point of order, in which he demanded that Foreign Minister Kyprianou be given the right to speak first. The President then took the opportunity to call upon Sir Patrick Dean to speak, at which point the United Kingdom's Permanent Representative restated the British belief that the Cypriot Foreign Minister should indeed have the opportunity to speak, but that it should come after the British address. At this point the Czechoslovak Representative took the opportunity to voice its support for the Soviet proposal. At the end, the President of the Council noted that under rule 27 of the procedure of the Council, 'The President shall call upon representatives in the order in which they desire to speak'. And that seeing as the British Representative had made his desire to speak first known first, then the floor was now given to him. For the verbatim account of this longwinded process see *United Nations Official Record of the Security Council*, 1095th Meeting, Tuesday 18 February 1964, S/PV.1095, paragraphs 4-32

41 Dean had actually made both an oral and a written request to the President of the Council to be allowed to speak first. The oral request was made at the end of the meeting held on the afternoon of Saturday, 15 February. See 'Record of Private Meeting of the Security Council at about 5 p.m. on Saturday, February 15, 1964.' *FO 371/174748*. It is worth noting that there was also a debate as to whether the Foreign Secretary should have been the one to handle the Security Council debate rather than Dean. For a full account of this see House of Commons, Official Report of Parliamentary Debates (*Hansard*), Fifth Series-Volume 689, Period 10th-21st February, 1964, pp.1031-1032.

42 *United Nations Official Record of the Security Council*, 1095th Meeting, Tuesday 18 February 1964, S/PV.1095, para.41

to move the matter to the Security Council. Dean then presented an overview of the current situation in Cyprus[43] before highlighting six points:

> First, the United Kingdom's actions in regard to the situation in Cyprus have throughout been within the framework of the Treaty of Guarantee.
> Second, the presence of British forces in the territory of Cyprus stems from an invitation by the Government of the Republic of Cyprus.
> Third, my government's efforts since the beginning have been directed to one end only - namely, to calming the situation and restoring peace.
> Fourth, my Government does not wish to continue to bear the burden of this peace-keeping operation alone for a day longer than necessary. It is for this reason that it has on several occasions made proposals for augmenting the peace-keeping force with contingents from other countries.
> Fifth, we have at all stages made it clear that our intention is to act with the agreement of the duly constituted authorities in Cyprus, and there had been no question of any proposals being implemented without such agreement.
> Sixth, the inability of the Government of the Republic of Cyprus to accept any of the proposals put to it, coupled with the recent and rapid deterioration in the situation in the island, makes it essential for this Council to be apprised of the situation and to take appropriate action.[44]

Dean explained that the first priority of the Council must be to restore peace on the island by 'substantially and rapidly' augmenting the peacekeeping force. To this end, the British Government had already prepared a draft resolution but would not present it at this stage as it was felt to be too premature.[45] However, the British representative made it clear that any resolution accepted should endorse the Secretary-General's appeal for calm, propose the establishment of a peacekeeping force at the first opportunity and appoint an impartial mediator. Moreover,

> The Council will no doubt wish to call on all States and authorities concerned to respect the independence, territorial integrity and security of the Republic of Cyprus, in accordance with the Treaty of Guarantee and as established and regulated by the basic articles of the Constitution.[46]

---

43 S/PV.1095, paras.66-75. The incidents highlighted included events at Khoulou village (Paphos area, 3 February), Ghaziveran (4 February), Ayios Sozomenos (7 February), Limassol (12 February), Ktima (13-14 February), Polis (14 February), and the discovery of weapons in Famagusta (15 February).

44 S/PV.1095, paras. 80-86

45 S/PV.1095, para. 93. This was presumably the same draft that had been shown to Bitsios.

46 S/PV.1095, para.94

Next to speak was Kyprianou.[47] Referring to Dean's presentation of the background history, he asked why,

> suddenly, at a certain stage in the history of Cyprus, there was inter-communal fighting, whereas for years in the past the people of Cyprus as a whole, whether Greek or Turk or Armenian or Maronite, have been living peacefully together without any incidents between them, and in fact, in the course of two world wars, Greeks and Turks in Cyprus were together on the same side of the Allies. So one is led to believe that the present situation in Cyprus – and we are quite convinced about it – is not the cause. The incidents which occur in Cyprus and which have been occurring recently are just symptoms of other causes.[48]

He continued by outlining the numerous threats posed by Turkey, and accused Ankara of pursuing an active policy of partition in Cyprus. Closing his speech, Kyprianou declared:

> As far as the Government of Cyprus is concerned, we are open to suggestions and ready for discussions both on the political solution of the problem and on the peace-keeping aspect of the problem within the framework of the United Nations. I must, however, make it clear that the territorial integrity, the unity, the sovereignty and the complete independence of our country are not negotiable. These are the very things we call upon the Security Council to safeguard and protect. We are an equal member of the United Nations, and we feel that we are entitled to this protection. We are confident that the Security Council will not fail us. If the fundamental elements which form the basis of the existence of the Republic of Cyprus are protected and the threat of aggression is done away with, peace in Cyprus can easily be restored. To this end, my Government is pledged to do its utmost, with the assistance of the Security Council.[49]

At this point Nikolai Fedorenko, the Permanent Representative of the Soviet Union called a point of order. He asked that, given the late hour, the Council might be allowed to adjourn to consider Kyprianou's comments in full. The request was rejected. Instead, the Turkish Representative was called to speak. Replying to Kyprianou, Turkey's acting-Representative, Turgut Menemencioglu,[50] started by explaining that the Greek Cypriot

---

47 Foreign Minister Kyprianou had decided to represent the Republic of Cyprus at the meetings of the Security Council. This was communicated in a 'Letter dated 17 February 1964 from the Minister for Foreign Affairs of Cyprus to the President of the Security Council', *United Nations Security Council Document*, S/5552. This acceptance of Kyprianou as the voice of the Republic of Cyprus at the Security Council made "a joke of the United Nations in the eyes of the Turkish Cypriots." Osman Orek, interview with the author.

48 S/PV.1095, para.98

49 S/PV.1095, para.145

50 Kyprianou states that Menemencioglu had in fact been the Turkish Ambassador in Washington at the time and had been called upon to lead the Turkish delegation at the United Nations because the Turkish Government "did not trust" its Permanent Representative to handle the debate. Spyros Kyprianou, interview

application to the Council was unconstitutional as it had been made without consulting Vice-President Kuchuk or the Turkish members of the Cabinet. In any case, the Turkish Representative firmly rejected the accusations that there had ever been a real Turkish military threat to Cyprus. Instead, the Greek Cypriots had used the forum of the United Nations in December as a means of diverting international attention away from the 'hideous crimes' that were taking place on the island.[51] Menemencioglu ended his speech by calling the Council's attention to the fact that the Turkish Government had done everything in its power to help stop the bloodshed and violence on the island, and that it had also shown remarkable restraint in the face of great provocations. He noted that Turkey would 'be at the side of any practical solution which can be found to this tragic situation'.[52]

The final speaker of the day was the Greek Representative, Dimitri Bitsios. Taking a stand that was broadly in favour of the Greek Cypriots, he nonetheless ensured that he did not alienate either the United Kingdom or Turkey. In fact, he gave what amounted to the most moderate speech of the day and pointed out that Cyprus was a state with both internal and external security difficulties. To this end,

> The three guaranteeing Powers and the Republic of Cyprus must pursue a single, common end – the restoration of order in Cyprus so that a basic solution to the problem may be sought, something which is not possible so long as the disorders continue and the threat of international conflict persists. Differences exist only as to method. We do not pretend to know the precise answers to all the questions before us. But we are certain that, whatever answers are given by the International Organization, before which the Cypriots have in full confidence placed their problems, they cannot but be in keeping with the letter and spirit of the Charter.[53]

Before closing the day's session, the President allowed Kyprianou to state that during the course of the debate, despite the Turkish Representative's assurances, the Turkish Minister of Information had in fact informed reporters that Turkey would intervene if the efforts at the United Nations failed. It was thus on an ominous note that the Council adjourned at twenty past seven in the evening.

The second day of discussions

Whereas the first day of the debate focused on the Greek Cypriots and the three Guarantor Powers, the second day was given over to the Superpowers. Ambassador Fedorenko, the

---

with the author. The Turkish Cypriots favoured Menemencioglu because of the fact that he was "an able diplomat" as well as figure "well known in Cyprus" and supported by the Turkish Cypriots. Osman Orek, interview with the author.

51 S/PV.1095, para.167. The Turkish representative then proceeded to give example of press accounts written at the time describing the situation with regard to the Turkish Cypriots. S/PV.1095, paras.168-175

52 S/PV.1095, para.230

53 S/PV.1095, para.254

first to speak, immediately introduced a Cold War element by noting a strong NATO presence in the region around Cyprus.[54] Criticising the United Kingdom directly, he chided the British Government for its 'intolerable lectures' to the Cypriot Government and claimed that the problems in Cyprus were the direct result of pressure on a small state from larger powers. Referring, albeit indirectly, to the Khrushchev letter, the Soviet Representative asked if sovereignty was, 'a right only to be possessed by the strong?'[55] Fedorenko then stated that Makarios had in fact been cajoled into accepting the Joint Truce Force as a *fait accompli* and that the later peacekeeping proposals had been aimed, 'with cynical frankness at nullifying the independence of the Republic of Cyprus, tying Cyprus to NATO and converting it to one of their military bridgeheads.'[56] He then indirectly accused the United Kingdom and the United States of having brought the matter to the UN by devious means.[57] Concluding his long speech, the Soviet representative called upon the Council to take 'urgent measures to protect the Republic of Cyprus from aggression and prohibit and stop any foreign intervention'.[58]

Although the floor was now due to have been given to Adlai Stevenson, Bernardes instead took note of a request by Dean to reply to Fedorenko. The British Representative emphasised that British troops were in Cyprus after having been invited there by the Cypriot Government and that their task was to 'restore tranquillity and normal condition' for all of the island's inhabitants. Moreover, and at great risk to themselves, they had 'saved numerous lives' and secured the release of many hostages. As a result, Sir Patrick noted that they had been praised by all concerned, especially as they had kept the peace without causing a single casualty. The British representative stressed that this was a record that Britain had a right to be proud of, despite the insinuations of the Soviet Representative.[59]

Fedorenko, deciding to reserve a reply until later, allowed the President of the Council to pass the floor to Stevenson. The American representative began his address by referring to the fact that the Treaty of Guarantee formed an integral part of the 'organic arrangements' that formed the Republic of Cyprus.[60] As far as Washington was concerned, the United States held no role in deciding what the final settlement of the Cyprus problem

---

54 *United Nations Official Record of the Security* Council, 1096th Meeting, Wednesday 19 February 1964, S/PV.1096, para.4

55 S/PV.1096, para.20

56 S/PV.1096, para.18

57 As Fedorenko stated: 'This undisguised manoeuvring brings to mind the ancient fable of how animal signs were invented for the zodiacal system of symbolic chronology. According to the fable, in the hour of trial, the Almighty summoned emissaries of the animal kingdom and they responded to His call. The honest ox was the first to set forth on the road and to arrive at the gates of Heaven, and so by rights he deserved to take precedence. But, to everyone's surprise, in front of the ox appeared a mouse, who had concealed itself inconspicuously in the ox's tail at the very beginning of the journey and suddenly jumped over the head of the animal at the gates of Heaven and in this way acquired undeserved honour.' S/PV.1096, para.39

58 S/PV.1096, para.56. This speech was well received across the Greek Cypriot political spectrum. See *Haravghi*, *Makhi*, *Eleftheria*, *Phileleftheros*, 20 February 1964.

59 S/PV.1096, paras. 60-62. When he was asked about Dean, Spyros Kyprianou noted that he "did not have any real complaints about him". However the distinct impression conveyed by this comment was that Kyprianou had not got on well the British Representative. Spyros Kyprianou, interview with the author.

60 S/PV.1096, para.74

should be and that, furthermore, neither it nor other western powers were attempting to impose their will on the Cypriot Government.[61] As for the earlier Soviet assertions of a NATO conspiracy, Stevenson simply replied,

> I shall not dwell at this time on the assertions of the representative of the Soviet Union whereby the anxiety that most of us have that peace must be restored to Cyprus is some form of NATO plot. No one is even proposing that the international force be comprised just of NATO military units. The parties will have to agree upon the participants in any such force.[62]

However, Stevenson did use the occasion to try to foster a continued spirit of Guarantor Power cohesion. Having by now taken a solid line in favour of the United Kingdom's position on the Treaty of Guarantee, the US Representative concluded:

> The United States values the spirit of co-operation which Greece and Turkey have shown in these dangerous weeks. They have demonstrated great restraint at a difficult moment in history. Both Governments, I believe, are to be commended for approaching Cyprus' problem, which has sensitive implications for both of them, with a sense of responsibility not only to the respective communities in Cyprus but also, more importantly, to the entire world community. We should be grateful to both of them.

At this point Bitsios took the floor and, in a comment that was remarkably partisan in light of the statement that Stevenson had just made, stated that the Greek Government believed that any solution reached by the Council would have to be acceptable to the Cypriots. While perfectly true, it was seen by the US as an unnecessary and provocative statement that was contrary to the interests of the Guarantor Powers.[63] In any case, the Council now adjourned for two days. It would next meet on Friday, 21 February.

U Thant attempts to mediate

Meanwhile, U Thant was trying to make progress in his attempts to secure Greek and Turkish support for a planned United Nations force. The following morning, 20 February, he had a second meeting with the Greek Cypriot delegates.[64] Over the course of ninety

61 S/PV.1096, para.78. Spyros Kyprianou, during an interview with the author, maintained that despite the differences between the Greek Cypriots and the United States Adlai Stevenson was "honest" and that they had a good relationship. Indeed, Kyprianou recounted a conversation between the two of them one day over lunch when Stevenson commented that had he been in a position to make the decision he would have handled the Cyprus matter differently from the way in which Washington had done so at the time.

62 S/PV.1096, para.79

63 The US Ambassador in Athens, Henry R. Labouisse, even confronted the new Greek Prime Minister, George Papandreou, about Bitsios' behaviour. Nicolet, *United States Policy Towards Cyprus, 1954-1974*, p.218

64 Clerides, *Cyprus. My Deposition* (Volume 2), p.53. The plan was also cited by *Reuters*, 20 February 1964

minutes of discussion the Secretary-General outlined the developments that had taken place since their last meeting. In particular, he noted that the plans for the force had been drawn up in such a manner as to put the Secretary-General in charge of the day-to-day control of the force, acting on the advice from the proposed three-man committee of members of the Security Council. This was not, however, an idea that was universally popular. Both the United States and the United Kingdom were against the creation of a committee on the grounds that there would be significant problems relating to its composition. Furthermore, the composition of the force would require the consent of the Republic of Cyprus. Both these points were liked by the Greek Cypriots as they secured a strong link to the Security Council and would ensure that no undesirable peacekeeping forces could be forced onto them. The Greek Cypriots also raised a query about the advisability of putting forward two separate proposals for a resolution, the first clarifying the territorial integrity of the Republic of Cyprus, and the second would focus on the formation of the force. U Thant promised to sound out the various members of the Security Council on these issues.

Commenting on the Turkish position, the Secretary-General explained that Turkey wished to see any clause relating to such territorial integrity include a specific clause referring to the rights of the Guarantor Powers. In addition Ankara believed that the 'Committee of Three' that would guide the Secretary-General should in fact be made up of the three Guarantor Powers. Additionally, the Turkish Government opposed the use of the term 'Republic of Cyprus' preferring instead the term 'Greek and Turkish communities of Cyprus'. However, U Thant believed that the Turkish Government would not press this latter point. More controversially, Turkey had also proposed creating a committee to investigate violations of the Convention on Genocide and the Convention on Human Rights.

The meeting adjourned with the Secretary-General agreeing to forward the results of the meeting to the other members of the Security Council. Indeed, later that same day U Thant had a joint meeting with the Norwegian Representative, Sievert Nielsen, and with US Representative Stevenson. This was followed by a 'private discussion' with Representative Menemencioglu of Turkey.

The next day the Greek Cypriots were called back to the UN Headquarters. However, this time they were surprised to find that the new proposals presented by U Thant were a step backwards from the ideas that they had been presented with the day before.[65] In particular, a lengthy preamble referring to the various Treaties was now proposed. In the course of the next five hours, another set of ideas was drafted that was more in tune with the Greek Cypriots' ideas. However, U Thant was now concerned that Turkey, which had not been happy about the earlier ideas, would flatly reject these. Indeed, the Secretary-General made it clear that in his view the only major point of difference between the parties lay with the Treaties. However, even on this issue there was some disagreement within the two camps over how a reference to the treaties should be handled. Ankara wanted a reference in the operational part of the resolution. On the other hand U Thant felt that

65 *Ibid.*, p.55

Britain and the United States would possibly be satisfied with some reference made in the preamble.

However, in light of the determination of the Greek Cypriots to avoid any mention of the Treaties, U Thant explained that he now saw little room for establishing common ground and that the debate before the Security Council should therefore continue.[66] However, even this would appear to be a fruitless undertaking. The Greek Cypriots had built up some support for their position from Moscow and so any debate seemed destined to develop along partisan, Cold War lines. Moreover, and by way of a further complication, the Soviet Union and Czechoslovakia had expressed the view that,

> (a) The question should be limited to a resolution calling all countries concerned to respect the territorial integrity, sovereignty, etc. of the Republic and to abstain from any threats or use of force in accordance with the Charter.
> (b) No reference should be made to the Treaties whatsoever.
> (c) No need exists for sending an international force to Cyprus.[67]

Given the state of the negotiations, the Council meeting was postponed that day.

The situation in Cyprus deteriorates further

Even though there had been a reduction in tensions on the island,[68] the deliberations taking place at the United Nations did little to ease either the overall political situation in Cyprus, or the problems faced by Britain as it attempted to keep the peace. The continued expansion of the Truce Force to meet the requirements of its ever more difficult job meant that a further one and a half thousand men were now on their way to Cyprus. Once they arrived there would be a total of six thousand British troops serving with the Truce Force, and another 3-4,000 in the Sovereign Base Areas.[69] All the while concern was growing at the increasing hostility being faced by the Truce Force from all sides. As one British newspaper reported at the time, the Greek Cypriot media was encouraging many to feel that Britain was trying to re-colonise the island and in doing so were favouring the Turkish Cypriots. However, the Turkish Cypriots were becoming increasing disillusioned with the Truce Force, which they felt was treating them badly.[70]

In a further attempt to limit the international presence on the island, Makarios now made it known that he wanted any international force created to be limited to 7,000 troops – three thousand below the figure previously produced for the NATO-based force.[71] At the

66 *Ibid.*, p.57
67 *Ibid.*
68 General Carver noted that the process at the United Nations had, 'to a certain extent lowered tension in the island, but tension could build up again quickly.' *Cyprus Mail*, 21 February 1964
69 *The Times*, 20 February 1964
70 *Ibid.*
71 *The New York Times*, 22 February 1964

same time, a decision was taken to the size of the Cyprus police force to around five thousand.[72] This decision was seen as being little more than an attempt to legitimize and arm a large number of Greek Cypriot irregulars. In the eyes of the United States all these steps, 'were aimed at replacing the British peace keeping forces before a UN replacement would be sent.'[73] This situation was all the more worrying given the reports emerging that Makarios was not wholly in control of the situation and that the two main Greek Cypriot militia leaders, Nicos Sampson and Interior Minister Polykarpos Yiorgadjis, were not only fighting the Turkish Cypriots but were also in competition against each other as well as Makarios.[74] With events threatening to spiral completely out of control at any time, the only positive piece of news – for Makarios, the United Kingdom, and the Turkish Cypriots – was a public statement by General Grivas that, contrary to expectations, he was not planning to return to Cyprus from Greece to resume his 'underground activities'.[75]

Meanwhile the possibility that events in Cyprus could still ignite a war between Greece and Turkey was still a very real danger and it appears as if proposals were being formulated within NATO to try to limit the chances of this happening. Speaking to a British official, the NATO Secretary-General, Dirk Stikker, claimed that he had been presented with an idea (he did not state by whom), 'that a NATO force might, with the agreement of both countries, be stationed across the Greco/Turkish border in Thrace, so as to keep the forces of the two countries apart.'[76]

The Security Council reconvenes

Back at the United Nations the situation could not have been worse. U Thant now reported that he was at an impasse regarding his attempts to mediate between the parties.[77] It was under this cloud that the Council reconvened at three thirty of the afternoon of 25 February. Opening the session, the President of the Council immediately passed the floor to the Secretary-General, who read the following personal statement:

> Since the last meeting of the Security Council, and, indeed, even before that meeting, I have had discussions with the parties principally involved for the purpose of exchanging views in an effort to clarify and define major issues...As

---

72 This move caused a certain degree of indignation and concern in the Turkish Cypriot community. Dr. Kuchuk immediately sent a cable to the President of the Security Council in which he alleged that the increase of the police directly violated Article 130 of the Cyprus Constitution and that it was a deliberate act designed 'to give a cloak of legality to Greek terrorist hordes which in fact number more than forty thousand according to a Greek minister'. See 'Text of Message sent by Dr. Kuchuk, Vice President of Cyprus, to the President of the Security Council on Makarios' Decision to establish additional security forces in Cyprus', *FO 371/174748*.

73 Nicolet, *United States Policy Towards Cyprus*, p.218

74 *The Economist*, 11 January 1964, p.104.

75 *The New York Times*, 23 February 1964

76 Letter from the United Kingdom Delegation to NATO to the Foreign Office Central Department, February 21, 1964, *FO 371/174748*

77 *Keesing's Contemporary Archives*, June 13-20 1964, p.20119

> you know, I have engaged in these informal discussion because it was clearly the wish of the parties that I should do so, and especially because in view of the seriousness and urgency of the Cyprus situation, it is my desire to do everything possible to help resolve this dangerous crisis...The discussions have been devoted primarily to expositions by the parties of their views of the problem and how it might be dealt with. It has not been my purpose to offer solutions, but as I said earlier, to seek common ground...I am convinced that there is an earnest desire on the part of all concerned to seek a peaceful solution, although, as may be expected, the positions on certain key issues have been firmly taken and maintained...may I express the hope that a reasonable and practical way out of the impasse will be found by this council. I will, of course, continue to be available and to do whatever may be appropriate in the circumstances to assist towards reaching a solution.[78]

For the first time since the debate had started, the chance to speak was given to one of the parties not directly involved with Cyprus. Noting that the independence of Cyprus had been 'welcomed by a number of friendly countries',[79] Sidi Baba, the acting representative of Morocco, went on to state that examples of the harmonious coexistence within a state could be found in many Arab countries and that once there was a mutual understanding of the need for peaceful coexistence within the state, the principle of independence and sovereignty should be accepted. To this end, the view of the Moroccan delegation was that, 'the less interference there is from abroad, the better it will be for the Cypriot people and the stability of its institutions.'[80] Morocco also considered that the terms of Cypriot independence, supported by the various treaties, could not be reconciled with the proper exercise of national sovereignty, especially in terms of a country that belonged to the United Nations and was also a member of the Non-Aligned Movement.[81]

The Greek Cypriots must surely have been pleased that the Moroccan was apparently leaning in their direction. However, it would have been short-lived satisfaction. Commenting on why the Turkish Cypriots, as a minority, might attach importance to the Zurich-London Agreements, Sidi Baba stated his hope that the Treaties would not be challenged 'abruptly and unilaterally', and that if changes were to be made it should be done through consensus between the communities 'in a spirit of national fraternity and respect for the rights of the communities.' If this could be achieved, or so the Moroccan argued, then it would deprive outside powers of an excuse to intervene.[82] Thanking the Secretary-General for his role, Sidi Baba said that he hoped that Cyprus would not become a 'theatre' for those forces traditionally bent on gaining a foothold in the Mediterranean and

---

78 *United Nations Press Release*, SG/SM/18, 25 February 1964
79 *United Nations Official Record of the Security Council*, S/PV.1097, para.12
80 S/PV.1097, para.14
81 S/PV.1097, para.15
82 S/PV.1097, para.22

that the Non-Aligned Movement was anxious to prevent the region from becoming exposed to the 'out-and-out competition of the Cold War'.[83]

The next to speak was the Norwegian Representative. As a representative of a NATO member state that had also expressed its interest in participating in the NATO-based force, Nielsen broadly took the side of the United Kingdom and declared his government's view that it was not a job for the Security Council to pronounce on the validity of the constitution of a member state, 'nor to pass judgement on a set of treaties which were negotiated as an integral part of the whole process of granting independence to that State.'[84] The Norwegian then made the first real move in the Council to address the question of a peacekeeping force and called upon all parties to cooperate with the Secretary-General without having any preconceived ideas about how this might be done. Concluding his address, Nielsen raised an important issue by pointing out that the view of the Norwegian Government was that any peacekeeping body established should be set up without financial obligations to the United Nations, especially given the state of the organisation's funding problems.[85]

The next to speak was Jiri Hajek, the representative of Czechoslovakia. Given the pro-Soviet Czech position up until this point, it came as no surprise when Hajek took almost exactly the same stance as Fedorenko. However, at the start of his speech he neatly, though with no uncertain bias, caught the dilemma facing the Security Council in its continued debate of the Cyprus issue:

> The present discussion on the question of Cyprus has so far produced two distinct points of view. On the one hand, the opinion has been voiced that our task is to ensure and strengthen the sovereignty, independence and territorial integrity of the Republic of Cyprus, which have been seriously threatened by interference and aggression from outside. On the other hand, we have witnessed an attempt to achieve through the United Nations a measure which would enable a group of States to interfere in the internal affairs of the Republic of Cyprus. These points of view are diametrically opposed to each other, and it is obviously extremely difficult, I am sorry to say, to find a compromise between them.[86]

Again elaborating the same views presented by Fedorenko, the Czech Representative finally added an interesting twist to his speech when he sought to parallel the situation in Cyprus with the events that befell his country in 1938,

83 S/PV.1097, para.32
84 S/PV.1097, para.39
85 S/PV.1097, para.44
86 S/PV.1097, para.47. When asked about the Czech Representative's performance at the United Nations, Spyros Kyprianou was full of praise for Hajek. Not only did he say that he had been "very supportive", but that his "brilliant interventions" had "explained the political and legal aspects of the whole question". Spyros Kyprianou, interview with the author.

> An aggressor from the outside used the leadership of an ethnical minority for unleashing disputes and conflicts and bringing about the disintegration of the State, for the purpose of furnishing alleged evidence that not only made the coexistence of that minority with the majority impossible, but also the very existence of Czechoslovakia untenable...In order to facilitate an agreement between the West and Hitlerite Germany, Czechoslovakia was continually asked and pressed to grant more and more concessions to the detriment of its sovereignty and security. It is interesting to note, for instance, that one of those demands urged a change be made in the Czechoslovak Constitution which, in effect, provided that the leadership of the minority, directed from abroad, would have been virtually able to block any political decision of the Government and open the door to intervention by the neighbouring State whenever suitable for it...In the name of peace, the Munich Diktat and the partition of the country was imposed upon Czechoslovakia, followed six months later by the occupation of Prague. Six months later the Second World War burst out.[87]

Comparing the situation in Cyprus to that which had befallen the Congo a few years earlier, Arsene Usher, the representative of the Ivory Coast,[88] noted that the United Nations should avoid any repetition of that case in Cyprus. As far as the situation regarding the Treaties was concerned, he acknowledged that international treaties should not be 'fixed or static' but that the unilateral abrogation of a treaty is bound to be a source of conflict and war.[89] Agreeing that a force should be created, Usher concluded that the sovereignty and territorial integrity of Cyprus should also be addressed in any final resolution.

Following the intervention of these three non-permanent members of the Council, the debate now returned to the parties with a direct interest. Taking the floor once again Menemencioglu replied to the Czech statement and made a somewhat veiled criticism of their policy of kowtowing to the Soviet Union. Continuing on, he criticised the relationship between the Czechs and the Slovaks in the Czechoslovak State,[90] and noted that although the Soviet Union had a Constitution that guaranteed the rights of many minorities, this had not made a 'sovereign identity'.[91]

Fedorenko, completely by-passing the Turkish comments, asked if he might be allowed to reply to the statement made by Sir Patrick Dean at the previous meeting. He again challenged the British assertion that Makarios invited the Guarantor Powers to intervene in December 1963, and accused the United Kingdom of the 'flagrant infringement

---

87 S/PV.1097, para.56. It is interesting to note that although there are a number of parallels that can indeed be drawn between the two cases, the whole presentation of the historical events cited by Representative Hajek displayed an interesting phenomenon, namely, how certain facets of history - especially with regard to inter-war events - were being presented in Communist countries at the time.

88 It is perhaps worth noting that the Ivory Coast's Ambassador to Cyprus had presented his credentials a month earlier on 25 January 1964. See the *Cyprus Mail*, 26 January 1964.

89 S/PV.1097, para.74

90 S/PV.1097, para.93

91 S/PV.1097, para.97

of the sovereignty of Cyprus.'[92] Moreover, he invited Dean to state categorically that Britain would not use 'armed force against Cyprus and that it intends, in the Cyprus situation, to abide strictly by its obligations as a State Member of the United Nations.'[93] Dean, in an effort to buy time, asked that Fedorenko's speech be translated into both English and French. At this point, Hajek called upon the President of the Council to be allowed to respond to the Turkish Representative's earlier statement. He used his response to give a detailed rebuttal to the comments and offered to send Menemencioglu a copy of the Czech Constitution to show that, 'the existence of the two national entities is fully respected.'[94] Sir Patrick Dean now replied to the earlier Soviet charges by asking the Soviet Representative to refer back to the six points that he had made in his address before the Council on the 18 February. By this stage the meeting had degenerated into little more than a series of accusations and counter-accusations. Little further progress seemed likely.

Kyprianou, taking the chance to thank the Secretary-General for his efforts to find a solution, and emphasising the important roles played by General Gyani and Rolz-Bennet, decided to focus his address on a discussion of the importance, or lack thereof, of the Treaty of Guarantee. More specifically, he argued that under Article 103 of the Charter of the United Nations, the instruction put before all members of the United Nations was:

> In the event of a conflict between the obligations of the Members of the United Nations under the Charter and their obligations under any other international agreement, their obligations under the present Charter shall prevail.

Kyprianou now threw down the gauntlet to the three Guarantor Powers. He called on each of them to clarify whether they felt they had a right to intervene militarily in view of the Charter provision he had just highlighted. Moreover, he called upon the Council to refrain from taking a final decision until Britain, Greece and Turkey had given an answer to his question.[95]

Following another attempt by Fedorenko to question Dean, Menemencioglu replied to Kyprianou's question by accusing the Greek Cypriots of hiding behind the United Nations to do away, 'with all their commitments, including treaties, and to give them the right to jump upon the remaining Turks, to finish what they have started.'[96] Kyprianou immediately responded that, 'As far as the exaggerations and distortions about genocide are concerned,

---

92 S/PV.1097, para.102

93 S/PV.1097, para.117

94 S/PV.1097, para.128

95 S/PV.1097, para.139

96 S/PV.1097, para.157. After further comments directed towards Kyprianou about the intentions of the Greek Cypriots towards the Turkish Cypriots there were interruptions - most probably from assembled Greek and Greek Cypriot citizens of the US - from the public gallery, at which point the Turkish representative said, 'Mr. President, will you please throw these savages out. This is not Limassol.' S/PV.1097, para.159. This incident was clearly remembered by Osman Orek and recounted during an interview with the author. In its report of the events the *Cyprus Mail* stated that the Turkish Representative had, 'withheld reply to a blunt question from Kyprianou.' *Cyprus Mail*, 27 February 1964. In criticising Kyprianou, Menemencioglu stated that the situation in Cyprus was, 'too tragic to use this kind of strategy.' *Cyprus Mail*, 27 February 1964

those are words which can be found more often in the vocabulary of his own country – and I am referring to the past, when unfortunately there was no Charter of the United Nations.'[97] To end the session, Bitsios stated that as far as the Greek Government was concerned the answer to Kyprianou's question was 'No'.[98] The Greek representative believed that intervention under the Treaty of Guarantee was indeed subject to authorization by the Security Council. With little further progress likely to be made, Bernardes called an end to the meeting at this point. He scheduled the return to the chamber for two days later, on 27 February.

97 S/PV.1097, para.164.
98 S/PV.1097, para.168

8

An Agreement is Reached

By now the main lines of division in the Council had become clear. While the Greek Cypriots could call on the support of the Soviet Union and Czechoslovakia, they faced opposition from the United Kingdom, Norway and the United States. The Ivory Coast and Morocco had taken a position that fell somewhere between the two respective camps. China had not spoken, nor had France, Brazil and Bolivia. Given that the Secretary-General was unable to find a solution, the split in the Council meant that chances of putting together an acceptable resolution therefore appeared to be minimal.

However, just as things appeared to be beyond hope, rumours emerged that five of the six non-permanent members of the Security Council, under the leadership of Carlos Bernardes, were about to introduce a new draft resolution for discussion. Regarding the specifics of the proposal, the following memorandum, written by an official attached to the Greek Cypriot delegation, showed the thinking behind the new move:

> Brazil's feeling is that the efforts of the Secretary-General did not result in complete failure and that if the matter was taken up from there and agreement was reached between the non-permanent Members, that agreement would be communicated to the parties concerned, with a view to minor modifications.
>
> At a meeting held yesterday evening a Paper was drafted containing a possible resolution. Three approaches were represented in the preamble. The first preamble contained no reference to either the integrity question or to the Treaties. The second draft preamble made clear reference to both the integrity question and to the Treaties. The third draft preamble made reference to both these issues in a diluted form.[1]

What was made clear from this note was that the main difficulties centred on the preamble of the resolution. The operative elements were settled. In analysing the three proposals, it was clear, on the basis of earlier arguments, that the first option, which made no mention of either the Treaties or the issue of territorial integrity, was going to be unacceptable to all parties. For the Greek Cypriots it did not provide an international guarantee against Turkish intervention. For Turkey and the United Kingdom it would not have established the

1 'Memorandum by Mr. A.J. Jacovides, re: Information obtained in a telephone conversation with Mr. Houaiss, Minister Plenipotentiary, Brazilian Mission, 25 February 1964.' This document is reprinted in Clerides, *Cyprus. My Deposition*, (Volume 2), p.62

fundamental importance of the Treaties. Options two and three were therefore going to be the most viable routes forward.

On Wednesday 26 February, the day following U Thant's statement, Bernardes informally distributed to the other members of the Council the first draft of the text of a resolution for the establishment of a United Nations force. During a meeting between Bernardes with the Greek Cypriots that same morning, the Greek Cypriot delegation expressed general support for the draft, seeing it as an attempt "to find something acceptable to everybody."[2] Indeed, Makarios, in spite of the certain difficulties with the wording of the resolution, appeared to be general supportive of the idea for a United Nations mediator and peace-keeping force. However, the exact nature of the proposed resolution continued to prove to be a sticking point.[3] As the Greek Cypriots noted, the proposed resolution failed,

> (a) To get Turkey specifically mentioned as the country towards which the admonition to respect the territorial integrity and sovereignty of the Republic of Cyprus, was directed.
> (b) To abrogate the Treaty of Guarantee.
> (c) To include as a term of reference of the Force to be stationed in Cyprus, either to defend Cyprus from aggression, or to prevent or restore the de facto situation created, or that which might be created in the future.[4]

Despite the fact that the proposed resolution failed to meet these points, the draft certainly met many of the overall aims of the Greek Cypriots. Indeed, by this point, the need to prevent a Turkish intervention was the main concern within the Greek Cypriot delegation. This was achieved by the resolution, which noted the island's territorial integrity issue. As Clerides later commented,

> The main shortcomings...of the resolution escaped the attention of the general public and the press. This was due to the fact that the attention of everyone was concentrated on the issue of removing the danger of military intervention by Turkey and not on the issue of abrogating the agreements.[5]

As the Greek Cypriots were satisfied with the proposed resolution, the Soviet Union, Czechoslovakia, and France all stated that they would support it.[6] French support for the draft was particularly interesting as Makarios was reported to have approached President de Gaulle to act as a mediator.[7] In an apparent attempt to break the deadlock, or perhaps to

2 Spyros Kyprianou, interview with the author.
3 *Keesing's Contemporary Archives*, June 13-20 1964, p.20119
4 Clerides, *op. cit.*, (Volume 2), p.78
5 *Ibid.*, p.78
6 *Ibid.*, p.76
7 *The Times*, 27 February 1964

break the Western unity,[8] the Archbishop had first suggested this idea publicly the previous day in an interview with *Le Monde*.[9] In Cyprus, pro-French feeling had grown over the previous week. On 16 February, *Makhi* had written that Makarios had decided to establish diplomatic representation in Paris at ambassadorial level,[10] and on the subject of a French mediating role, a commentary written in the newspaper *Ethniki* had suggested that de Gaulle would be the 'ideal neutral mediator.'[11] However, there seemed little danger that France, a view supported by the United States.[12] Nonetheless, the reports worried London given the radical views on the Cyprus problem that de Gaulle had allegedly expressed in the past. In particular, the General had been reported to have mentioned the possibility of a large-scale repatriation of the island's Turkish community[13] – a proposal that no doubt contributed to the Greek Cypriot view of the General as an ideal mediator. However, the panic soon died down. French Government officials soon denied knowledge of an official request for mediation.[14] The idea did not surface again as a serious proposal.

Britain persuades the US to accept the draft resolution

However, while the draft may have been acceptable to the Greek Cypriots and their allies, it still needed approval from Britain, Turkey and the United States. As far the British Government were concerned, they 'did not see any alternative to supporting the Resolution which the Five are proposing.'[15] Although the text went a considerable way towards the Greek Cypriot aim of having the independence and territorial integrity of Cyprus recognised, it nonetheless made direct reference to the Treaty of Guarantee. Moreover, and importantly, it did not specifically refer to Turkey. London therefore requested that David Bruce, the US Ambassador in London, convey the view that Washington should not only accept the resolution but that they should assist the British Government by trying to persuade the Turkish Government to accept the draft.[16]

Later that same day, however, Bruce contacted the Foreign Office to explain that the United States was unwilling to accept the draft resolution as it stood because, 'it would be unacceptable to the Turks.'[17] The sticking point, as far as the US was concerned, was that the preamble of the proposed resolution referred to the sovereignty and territorial integrity of the Republic of Cyprus. Despite this initial reply, further discussions between the British Ambassador, Sir David Ormsby Gore, and George Ball in Washington led to a rethink of

8 *Cumhurriyet*, 29 February 1964
9 *Le Monde*, 26 February 1964
10 *Makhi*, 16 February 1964
11 *Ethniki*, 23 February 1964
12 *Reuters*, 5 February 1964
13 Letter from the United Kingdom's delegation to NATO Paris to the Central department of the Foreign Office, February 27, 1964, *FO 371/174748*
14 *The New York Times*, 28 February 1964
15 Memorandum dated 28 February 1964, *FO 371/174748*
16 *Ibid.*
17 *Ibid.*

the US position. The US Administration decided that they would not oppose the resolution simply because, 'the Turks disliked it'. Sandys explained that the US rethink was,

> comforting to a point, although it probably meant that they [the United States] would now try to manoeuvre so there was objection to the Resolution from the Greek or Greek-Cypriots as well as the Turks. I said that, before the Americans went ahead on this line, they must understand that we saw no, repeat no, alternative compromise to a resolution on the lines now under discussion. If this were to fail, the result would not be a meeting of the three Guarantor Powers. Sir P. Dean said that he fully understood this, and that the most likely next step would be a meeting of the Assembly, which everyone in their senses wished to avoid.[18]

The Greek Government changes

Meanwhile, without realising by this point that the draft resolution was basically acceptable to the Greek Cypriots, London was also growing increasingly worried that the draft resolution would be rejected not only by the Turkish Government but also by the Greeks.[19] To this extent, London suggested a meeting between the two men, even though it felt that the new Greek Prime Minister, George Papandreou, and Prime Minister Inonu would be unlikely to agree to meet to discuss the matter without some form of 'third party invitation and a juridical excuse for conferring.'[20] However, Ball rejected the idea and instead suggested that some form of conference might succeed if it were done under the auspices of the provisions of the Treaty of Guarantee.[21] As Ball commented,

> I feel more than ever that some move of this kind [a meeting of the Guarantor Powers] is imperative. It seems evident that the Greek Cypriot game is to keep the United Nations proceedings going. This is a forum where they can draw support from their Communist friends. It provides them with insulation against a Turkish move while eroding Turkish intervention rights.[22]

Moreover, the idea of a meeting of the Guarantor Powers seemed, to the United States at least, to have afforded the following opportunities:

---

18 *Ibid.*

19 C.M.15 (64), 27 February 1964, *CAB 128/38*

20 Message from Undersecretary Ball to the Foreign Secretary, R.A. Butler and the commonwealth Secretary, Duncan Sandys, dated 27 February 1964, *FO 371/174748*

21 What was not known by London was that Ball had actually wanted to try to call Greece and Turkey together to meet, but to do so without London. However, by the point Ball was approached by the British with this 'new' idea for a meeting, he was able to inform Britain that the idea, 'had already been explored and was dead.' Nicolet, *United States Policy Towards Cyprus, 1954-1974*, p.217

22 Message from Undersecretary Ball to the Foreign Secretary, R.A. Butler and the commonwealth Secretary, Duncan Sandys, dated 27 February 1964, *FO 371/174748*

> (a) To convince Makarios that the Turks mean business and that he is playing too risky a game;
> (b) To press Makarios to accept and support a peace-keeping force along the lines of the Thant plan; and
> (c) To undertake contingency planning for a possible tripartite intervention as an alternative to unilateral Turkish move.[23]

By the following day, however, the British Government had completely ruled out another meeting of the Guarantor Powers on the grounds that the Greek Government would almost certainly refuse to attend.[24] This was in large part due to the worrying change of position that Athens had adopted following the election of George Papandreou. Rather than the weak caretaker government led by Paraskevopoulos, Papandreou was at the helm of an administration that had won a convincing victory in the polls. And even though Papandreou had welcomed the initial British intervention in Cyprus back in December, he had nonetheless campaigned on a platform that, amongst other things, opposed the Zurich-London Agreements.[25] It came as little surprise when his victory led to large, and violent, anti-British and anti-American demonstrations in Athens.[26]

That same day, the new Greek Foreign Minister announced that he was re-examining Athens Radio broadcasts of Greek language BBC World Service and Voice of America (VOA) news items on the basis that such accounts were 'unfavourable' to Cyprus.[27] This was followed, the next day, by a ban all BBC broadcasts, followed the day after with a ban on the VOA and the French RDF service. At the same time the new government also issued a stern warning to Turkey.[28] Stavros Kostopoulos, the new Greek foreign minister, summoned the Turkish Ambassador to inform him that that, 'if Turkey decided to make a unilateral intervention in Cyprus, Greece would intervene.'[29] However, Turkey did not overact to developments taking place in Greece. Instead, in a statement to the press, Prime

---

23 *Ibid.* Ball ended his message with the following comment, 'I think it very likely that if the Security Council fades out and the Cypriots prove unable to secure an emergency General Assembly meeting the present superficial calm will give way to a bloodbath.'

24 Memorandum dated 28 February 1964, *FO 371/174748*

25 *Cyprus Mail*, 19 February 1964

26 It is interesting to note that despite the fiercely anti-NATO demonstrations that had taken place earlier in Athens during which there had been a strong show of support for the Soviet Union, the percentage of the vote taken by the United Democratic Left, the 'legal cover' party of the Communists (who were still banned by law), actually fell from around 25% in the 1958 elections to around 11% (22 of the 300 seats) in the February 1964 election.

27 *Reuters*, 25 February 1964

28 'Greece...warned all neighbouring countries that the Greek armed forces had received instructions to shoot down any foreign plane intruding into her air space.' *Cyprus Mail*, 18 February 1964. A factor closely linked to the continuing tensions with Turkey over the Cyprus issue.

29 *The Times*, 29 February 1964. Soon afterwards a report on Kostopoulos appeared in a Turkish newspaper in which it was claimed that the new Greek foreign minister was, 'a close friend of Grivas and responsible for encouraging EOKA and Enosis' *Tercuman*, 3 March 1964

Minister Inonu said that Turkey would try 'all imaginable measures' to avoid the 'last resort' of intervention in Cyprus.[30]

On 27 February, Papandreou informed the Ambassadors of Britain and the United States that his government had decided to support Makarios and would help him to restore the 'peace and the principles of democracy' in Cyprus.[31] At the same time Papandreou told the Greek people in an address that the, 'Greek Government gives its unqualified assistance to the just struggle of Cypriot Hellenism...[and that the] tragic consequences of the Treaties of London and Zurich are now being revealed.'[32] These events were a blow to Britain and the United States. Whereas previously Makarios had only been able to rely on the full support of the Soviet Union and Czechoslovakia in the Security Council, he now also had the complete support of the Greek Government.

The Security Council meets again

The Greek Cypriots were now in a stronger position than at any time since the crisis had erupted. In addition to their support from the Soviet Union, Czechoslovakia, France and Greece, Ball also noted that the Greek Cypriots were having some success with their efforts to gain support from Morocco and the Ivory Coast, both of which had previously seemed to be 'neutral' from their respective speeches at the Security Council.[33]

It was under these circumstances that the Security Council reconvened on the afternoon of Thursday 27 February.[34] The first item of discussion was a letter submitted by the Turkish Permanent Representative on 19 February requesting that Rauf Denktash, the President of the Turkish Cypriot Communal Chamber, be allowed to address the Council,[35] and which had been followed up by a letter from Denktash himself calling the Security Council's attention to the events taking place on the island.[36]

Opening the session, the Soviet Representative quickly rejected the application, stating that the Council had already listened to the arguments of the accepted delegation from Cyprus and that it should not try to isolate the Cypriot Government, either diplomatically or politically. Next to respond to the request was Dey Ould Sidi Baba , the permanent representative of Morocco. Though voicing sympathy with the Republic of Cyprus, he supported the application on the grounds that it would allow a full and proper discussion on

30 *Reuters*, 27 February 1964

31 *Reuters*, 27 February 1964

32 *Cyprus Mail*, 1 March 1964. Tassos Papadopoulos, in an interview with the author, noted that not only did the new Papandreou administration support the Greek Cypriots it also had a clear policy on Cyprus.

33 Message from Undersecretary Ball to the Foreign Secretary, R.A. Butler and the commonwealth Secretary, Duncan Sandys, dated 27 February 1964, *FO 371/174748*. Indeed, as Clerides noted, 'While the President of the Security Council was busy negotiating the second draft of his resolution with the non-permanent members of the Security Council, we were busy talking with them, in particular to Bolivia, Morocco and the Ivory Coast in an effort to get them to propose certain amendments.' Clerides, *op. cit.*, (Volume 2), p.74

34 *United Nations Official Record of the Security Council*, S/PV.1098

35 *United Nations Security Council Document*, S/5556

36 *United Nations Security Council document*, S/5561. A reprint of this letter can be found in Moran (ed.) *Rauf Denktash at the United Nations*, pp.4-5

the Cyprus issue by the Council.'[37] Third to speak was Castrillo Justiniano, the Bolivian Representative, who took the Soviet view and also argued that granting a hearing to the Turkish Cypriot delegate could be viewed as an infringement of the United Nations' principle of non-interference in the domestic jurisdiction of states. Yet, in a move that indicated that his Government was open to such a move if the Council so wished, he asked that the President clarify the exact issue at stake if the Turkish Cypriots wanted to address the Council.[38] After another brief interjection by the Soviet representative, the President asked that the Council make a formal proposal, under Security Council Rule of Procedure 39. Following some further procedural debates, the Council decided to call upon Denktash to address the Council at its next meeting, but on the condition that he do so as a private individual and not as the representative of the Turkish Cypriots.[39]

Before adjourning, the Council still had several matters that it needed to address and there were a number of speakers listed to participate that day. The first speaker was Sir Patrick Dean. Referring to the question concerning the Treaty of Guarantee vis-à-vis the Charter of the United Nations, which had been asked by Kyprianou at the previous meeting, Dean noted that provisions were made, under Article 51, for the use of force.[40] In addition, Article IV of the Treaty of Guarantee did not permit the use of force unilaterally, but instead allowed for, 'the right to take action with the sole aim of re-establishing the state of affairs created by the present Treaty.' Furthermore, Sir Patrick stressed that it was not the task of the Council to consider hypothetical questions, which, 'if the Government of Cyprus and all other Governments concerned do their duty, will remain hypothetical for ever.'[41]

However, Dean's most important statement came immediately afterwards when he announced that the British Government had not sent its troops to Cyprus under the terms of Article IV of the Treaty of Guarantee, but had done so because those forces had been asked for and because they were 'generally considered necessary and helpful in preventing further serious strife.'[42] Continuing, Dean made another important point:

> When I spoke last week [1095th meeting], I warned the Council that for any one nation to carry the main responsibility of peace-keeping is, at the least, unwise. Events since then have underlined the dangers of this and the need for an international force. My Government is prepared to take such part as may be

37 S/PV.1098, para.7
38 S/PV.1098, para.10
39 S/PV.1098, paras. 61-62
40 S/PV.1098, para.65
41 S/PV.1098, para.69
42 S/PV.1098, para.79. Bitsios notes of this moment in the debate '...the Foreign Minister of Cyprus asked point blank the representatives of Britain, Greece and Turkey, whether they considered that the Treaty of Guaranty [sic] conceded to their Governments the right to intervene unilaterally in Cyprus. The Turkish Representative, rather annoyed, said that he had answered that question in one of his previous speeches. My answer was categorically negative. The Council was waiting to hear the British view: it could tip the balance. Sir Patrick skilfully sidestepped the issue: "The British Troops" he said, "presently on Cypriot territory, are not there under the provisions of the Treaty of Guaranty". The tension subsided and the debate was allowed to proceed in a more relaxed atmosphere.' Bitsios, *Cyprus. The Vulnerable Republic*, p.148

> thought appropriate in an international force properly constituted, but I must warn the Council that it is neither helpful nor fitting for us to continue alone to carry out this thankless task if there is no prospect of an international force or steps towards an agreed solution of the problems of Cyprus.[43]

These two points were absolutely vital. In the first instance, by stressing that the Joint Truce Force was not an imposed intervention force placed in Cyprus by the Guarantor Powers, the British Representative was in fact reserving the rights of the Guarantor Powers to intervene at a later stage. Coupled with London's declared intention to withdraw its troops if no suitable resolution could be found,[44] Sir Patrick Dean had just threatened the Greek Cypriots with the possibility of direct intervention by Turkey if they tried to prevent an acceptable resolution. Yet, in a politically masterful stroke, Dean had also made an intervention politically dangerous for Turkey, as it would now have to invoke the Treaty of Guarantee – a move that had, on the basis of Dean's previous comment, clearly not been done by this point.[45] In effect, Dean had just emphasised to both the Greek Cypriots and to Turkey the importance of accepting the presented draft resolution.

Kyprianou, seemingly ignoring this vital speech, instead chose to make made another effort to try to produce a definite answer to his earlier question and noted that there had been a number of improvements in the situation in Cyprus since the Council had taken up the issue. The improvement had resulted in a limited amount of Greek-Turkish Cypriot co-habitation in a number of areas.[46] According the Cypriot Foreign Minister, this easing of tensions was a direct result of the reduced fears on the island over an external intervention.

At the end of Kyprianou's statements, Ambassador Seydoux presented France's position in the Council for the first time. After the various rumours that had circulated about a possible French role in the crisis as a mediator, Seydoux made a fairly short speech in which he seemed to disassociate France from the Greek Cypriots by noting that despite the tragic state of affairs in the island the Security Council had no right to interpret the agreements forming the Republic of Cyprus.[47] Instead, the duty of the Council was to urge the two communities and the Government of Cyprus to exercise restraint.

The Bolivian representative then followed and also took the chance to give a more comprehensive account of his Government's view of the situation than had been given in his earlier address. Noting some parallels between his country and Cyprus, Justiniano noted that a small state such as Cyprus with only limited military power had no option but to seek the 're-negotiation or revision of unjust treaties.'[48] Indeed, referring to events in the

---

43 S/PV.1098, para.82

44 This comment became the headline of the *Cyprus Mail* on 28 February 1964. However, in Turkey there was a general feeling that, 'Britain was not likely to withdraw its troops.' *Milliyet*, 29 February 1964.

45 Nonetheless, *Milliyet*, citing sources at the Turkish Foreign Ministry, noted that if the United Kingdom chose to withdraw, 'Turkey will not hesitate to use its intervention rights.' *Ibid.*

46 S/PV.1098, para.117

47 *Ethniki* (1 March 1964) and *Eleftheria* (3 March 1964), both expressed disappointment at France's attitude in the Security Council.

48 S/PV.1098, para.159

Americas, the Bolivian drew the Council's attention to press reports that very morning referring to the fact that the United States was about to renegotiate the 1903 Treaty with Panama. Concluding, Justiniano restated his support for Cyprus' desire to have the Treaties reviewed, but also expressed clear agreement with the United Kingdom's desire to see a peacekeeping force put in place.[49]

At this point Menemencioglu again stressed his Government's view that the Treaties were important documents that were needed to secure the vital interests of a number of countries, and that they had been signed on that basis. However, given the situation in Cyprus, the Turkish representative noted that the most pressing task of the Council was the issue of a peacekeeping force. In reply, Kyprianou accused Menemencioglu of calling for partition, and stated that while Makarios had indeed signed the various agreements, this did not mean that he had signed them willingly.[50] After a further, brief comment by Bitsios during which he took note of the fact that Menemencioglu had called Kyprianou the representative of the Greek Cypriots, rather than the representative of the Government of Cyprus, the meeting came to an end.

The meeting had again exposed the deep divisions within the Council as to how the Cyprus situation should be handled. However, it was by no means an unproductive meeting. The trend of the debate had shown that the Council was decidedly unwilling to pronounce on the validity of the Treaty of Guarantee. On the other hand, it was also becoming more obvious that there were positive moves towards the idea that the sovereignty, independence and territorial integrity of the island should be addressed within the draft resolution.

Denktash presents the Turkish Cypriot position

Importantly, it now seemed as if the Greek Cypriots were on the verge of being recognised by the international community as the Government of Cyprus, with or without the continued role of the Turkish Cypriots. The final chance for the Turkish Cypriot community to avoid this recognition now lay with Rauf Denktash. His appearance before the Council on the following day would in many ways determine the final shape of a Security Council resolution.

It was within this context that the members of the Council reconvened the next afternoon, 28 February, to hear the Turkish Cypriot representative speak in a personal capacity. As had been the case the day before, the session opened with a demand by the Soviet Representative to call a point of order. This time he asked Menemencioglu to clarify the point raised by Bitsios at the last meeting regarding the Turkish representatives insistence on referring to Kyprianou as a Greek Cypriot representative, rather than the Cypriot Minister of Foreign Affairs. The Turkish Representative drew Fedorenko's attention to the fact that on foreign affairs matters decisions could only be taken after a

49 S/PV.1098, para.165 & 167
50 S/PV.1098, para.186

meeting of the Council of Ministers of Cyprus, and then only with the agreement of both the President and Vice-President of the Republic. Seeing as this had not been done 'it is only natural for me to say that these opinions [presented by Kyprianou at the Council] reflect only the opinion of those who made them.'[51] The Soviet Representative, not content with the answer, launched into a rant about the way in which important rules of protocol had been ignored.

Once this outburst was over, Bernardes called upon Kyprianou to address the Council. He started by taking Fedorenko's lead, noting that Menemencioglu's insulting behaviour was not directed at himself but at the Security Council as an institution. Responding, the Turkish Representative simply stated that he had presented his case and would henceforth cease to participate in debates of this kind, especially as the Soviet Union was attempting to separate the interested parties. Yet again Fedorenko tried to call Menemencioglu to account for his statement. And yet again the Turkish Representative made no move to answer. At this point, Bernardes called upon Denktash to address the Council.

Denktash immediately launched into a bitter attack on the Greek Cypriots in general, and Archbishop Makarios in particular. Drawing the Security Council's attention to the continued fighting in Cyprus, Denktash questioned the intentions of the Greek Cypriots to see a United Nations' peacekeeping force put in place.[52] He then explained his views on Greek and Turkish Cypriot cohabitation in Cyprus:

> Turks and Greeks have lived in Cyprus together since 1571. They have so lived always as Greeks or Turks. They have each stuck to their separate culture, religion, tradition and national heritage. They are in effect Turkey and Greece projected into Cyprus for the Turkish and Greek populations respectively. Any attempts to make them anything but Greeks or Turks have met with strong opposition from these groups in Cyprus. They have lived as autonomous communities together, yet always separate. Down to the smallest village there have always been, and there is, Greek and Turkish authorities looking after the affairs of their communities separately. As long as they enjoyed equality and justice, they lived together happily. As soon as one side attempted to dominate the other politically, trouble brewed and their relations were momentarily estranged.[53]

The speech then continued with an account of the period leading to independence, before moving on to present a number of examples that sought to show that the Greek Cypriots saw independence as a transition stage that would eventually lead to full union with Greece, thus rendering the Turkish Cypriots a small minority. It was this state of affairs, he argued, that had led to the outbreak of fighting.

---

51 S/PV.1099, para.13
52 S/PV.1099, para.46
53 S/PV.1099, para.56

Attempting to present the Turkish Cypriots in a more conciliatory light, Denktash then read out a letter written a few days earlier by Vice-President Kuchuk to President Makarios in which the Turkish Cypriot leader had attempted to highlight the numerous mistakes that the Archbishop had made regarding his policy vis-à-vis the Turkish Cypriot community.[54] Through the use of a 'propaganda machine', the impression of the Turkish Cypriots that had been conveyed to the international community by the Greek Cypriots was one of a rebellious minority, and not of partners in the Republic of Cyprus. As a result of this effort, Denktash argued that the Security Council had failed to realise the vital importance of ensuring that the Constitution, and therefore the Treaty of Guarantee, could not be abrogated or amended.[55] Following on from this, the Turkish Cypriot categorically denied a plot designed to bring about partition in Cyprus. However, in his final words he said,

> Today no constitution is in effect in Cyprus. None of the provisions of the Constitution are being complied with or applied. In the circumstances which have been created it cannot be applied. So the two communities have fallen apart. It is not the fault of Mr. Kyprianou that he has not been able to get full instructions from Dr. Kuchuk and the Turkish Ministers to have this discussed fully in the Ministerial Council. The Greek gunmen will not let the Turks go to the other side and the ministerial function is finished. But with due respect to him, I do not think he can say or that he can claim in justice and fairness and humanity that he can represent the Turkish voice, that he can fully represent the Turkish side in this Council. He cannot'[56]

The Security Council debate continues

While most expected Kyprianou to respond to Denktash's allegations, the Cypriot Minister instead chose to hold off giving a reply.[57] By now, all the interested parties had presented their various views on the situation and it was becoming obvious that the greater proportion of the Council wished to bring the matter to a conclusion and vote on a resolution.

As a note of warning, Liu Chieh of China stated that despite the complexity of the Cyprus situation, the Security Council must refrain from becoming a judicial rather than a political body.[58] Following this, Bitsios thanked both the Secretary-General and the President of the Security Council for their 'untiring efforts...to reconcile diverging views

---

54 S/PV.1099, paras.69-70. The letter was submitted to Makarios on 19 February 1964.

55 This raises an important point about the extent to which the Treaty of Guarantee represents an integral part of the Constitution of the Republic of Cyprus. If it is considered to be part of the constitution then it is not, technically, able to be opened for discussion by the United Nations as it is essentially a domestic matter - unless, of course, it is brought to the Council's attention by the Government of Cyprus. Therefore, by merely recognising an issue in the Treaty of Guarantee, it could be argued that the Council, whether intentionally or otherwise, recognised the Greek Cypriots as the Government of Cyprus.

56 S/PV.1099, para.99

57 Spyros Kyprianou, interview with the author.

58 S/PV.1099, para.107

and to work out procedures which, with due regard for the interests of the parties involved in the Cyprus question, might cope constructively with the extreme gravity of the situation we are considering.'[59] He then presented the two views originally brought before the Council, and noted that the Greek Cypriots had justified their claim against Turkey. He finished by criticising Denktash as a man 'whose personal responsibility for the difficulties Cyprus now faces and in recent years has had to face is...heavy'.[60]

Kyprianou now spoke. Rather than replying to Denktash, he announced that he wanted to refer back to the situation in Cyprus. In particular he explained that the Council should be made aware that although there was calm on the island, Cyprus was again under a threat of attack from Turkey. As far as the proposed resolution was concerned, the foreign minister stated,

> I am confident that, if the Security Council decides to protect the territorial integrity and the independence of Cyprus, peace will be restored in the island. As we have said on various occasions, in order to allay certain fears – which we believe have no basis – we do not object in principle to having an international force under the United Nations. Some people have tried to say that we have attempted by tricks to avoid having such a force. We feel that, if Cyprus is protected, a force is not necessary – but nevertheless we are prepared to have it. However, having a force is not the goal. Having a force is one of the means towards the restoration of normal conditions and order. You cannot have a force there to restore normal internal conditions for a period of three months – and yet have Turkey feel that it has the right to intervene whenever it likes. You will not thereby be serving any purpose.[61]

Given the tensions of the session, Menemencioglu decided to adopt a more conciliatory tone. He stressed that Turkey had no territorial claim on Cyprus, and that Turkey, as a founder of the Republic of Cyprus, wished to see it prosper.[62] Importantly, the Turkish Representative drew the Council's attention to the fact that the issue brought before the Council by the Greek Cypriots was the need to have the territorial integrity, and the like, of Cyprus respected and for the Treaty of Guarantee to be abrogated, and yet, under Article II of the Treaty:

> Greece, Turkey and the United Kingdom, taking note of the undertakings of the Republic of Cyprus set out in Article I of the present Treaty, recognize and guarantee the independence, territorial integrity and security of the Republic of Cyprus

59 S/PV.1099, para.110
60 S/PV.1099, para.115
61 S/PV.1099, para.127
62 S/PV.1099, para.131

In other words, these issues were, in the view of the Turkish Government, redundant. He emphasised this point by stating that, 'Turkey has never said that it feels free to invade or intervene whenever it sees fit.'[63]

Kyprianou therefore asked the Turkish Representative if he would therefore object to having such phraseology used within the text of a resolution. Menemencioglu refused to answer directly,[64] stating that his earlier comment was on record and that he accepted responsibility for his comments. Bitsios now chimed in by noting that there could no longer be any difficulty with this clause as Turkey had already recognised it – a point picked up by the Soviet Representative who again asked the Turk for a direct answer. Menemencioglu stood firm and again drew the Council's attention to his earlier statement. Fedorenko, unwilling to let the matter drop, again pushed for a reply. Kyprianou, seeing the pointlessness of this, now tried a different approach. He asked whether, given that the Turkish Government had already made clear that the Treaty of Guarantee was in accordance with the Charter of the United Nations, and that Cyprus was a member of the United Nations, it would really be difficult for the Turkish member to accept a resolution calling for the sovereignty, and the like, of Cyprus to be accepted. Oblivious to the subtlety of the point made by Kyprianou, Fedorenko once more asked for a direct response. This ruined the moment. Menemencioglu reverted to his standard response and pointed out that he had answered this question twice.[65] The President of Council now called the meeting to an end, scheduling the next session for the afternoon of Monday 2 March.

The resolution of the five non-permanent members

It was now obvious that the political situation within the Security Council was such that no particular party was going to get all their demands met within a resolution. Given Menemencioglu's comment, it seemed as if the Turkish Government had, by this point, accepted that it would have to put up with a resolution that called upon unspecified states to respect the sovereignty, independence and territorial integrity of Cyprus, but which would also recognised the current validity of the various Treaties signed in 1960 – especially the Treaty of Guarantee.[66] At the same time, Britain and the United States would get a peacekeeping force put in place without alienating Turkey in the process. The Greek Cypriots, although unhappy with these points, were nonetheless satisfied insofar as they were about to be recognised as the effective Government of Cyprus. Moreover, in the

---

63 S/PV.1099, para.135

64 Kyprianou notes the way in which the Turkish Representative made a number of attempts to avoid the question, and stated that it was not difficult for him to argue with the Turkish Representative for no other reason than the fact that Menemencioglu had "no arguments". Spyros Kyprianou, interview with the author.

65 S/PV.1099, para.156

66 One of the reasons why the Turkish Government may have so readily accepted the Resolution, despite its problems, lay with the fact that Inonu's personal envoy to advise the Turkish delegation, Professor Nihat Erim (who later became a Turkish Prime Minister), was known to have favoured the terms presented in the draft. Osman Orek, personal interview with the author.

process of recognition they had made a military intervention significantly more difficult for Ankara.

This therefore left the Turkish Cypriots. Their prime concern was to avoid having any resolution put in place that would recognise the Greek Cypriots as the Government of Cyprus. Not wanting the Turkish Cypriots to delay the passage of the resolution any longer, London and Washington, with the knowledge and blessing of the Turkish Government,[67] asked that the Turkish Cypriot community's concern about the question of recognition be put to one side for the meanwhile. In return, Britain and the United States would ensure that once the resolution had been passed they would continue to press for the Turkish Cypriot case.[68] Although this promise is now regarded by the Turkish Cypriots as having been a lie,[69] it was on the basis of this commitment that the Turkish Cypriot leadership, pressured by Turkey,[70] agreed to co-operate.[71] The final major difficulty had now, apparently, been overcome.

On 2 March, the Security Council met again. The Presidency of the Council had by this point rotated and Liu Chieh had replaced Bernardes. After thanking the Brazilian representative for his efforts over the previous month,[72] Liu passed on to the substantive matter of the day, the presentation of a draft resolution to the Council. This document was the final version of the proposal that had been formulated by five of the six non-permanent members of the Security Council – Bolivia, Brazil, the Ivory Coast, Morocco, and Norway (the exception was Czechoslovakia). Liu Cheih therefore gave the floor to Bernardes to explain the thinking behind the draft:

> My colleagues and I, benefiting from the groundwork laid by the Secretary-General, are thus in a position to put before the Council a draft resolution which we consider to be a fair and balanced document. This draft is the result of lengthy negotiations, much give-and-take and compromise, and if it fails to give entire satisfaction to any of the parties concerned - and this may be its greatest value – we earnestly believe that it will not be unacceptable to them.[73]

At this point the Brazilian took the chance to run through the document and explain each of the seven paragraphs that made up the proposed resolution, the main aim of which was to prevent any fighting that might threaten international peace and security. To this end, the draft resolution would, under operational paragraph 4,

---

67 Necati Ertekun, personal interview with the author.
68 Rauf R. Denktash and Osman Orek, personal interviews with the author.
69 Osman Orek, personal interview with the author.
70 Foreign Minister Erkin of Turkey is claimed to have told the Turkish Cypriots 'not to play on words', as the delay would mean more 'Turkish blood would be spilled'. Necati Ertekun, interview with the author.
71 Rauf R. Denktash, interview with the author. Necati Ertekun, states that the Turkish Cypriots went along with the deal as they felt that the United Nations could deal with the immediate situation, but that despite this they never gave up hope that Turkey would intervene if necessary. Necati Ertekun, interview with the author.
72 1100th meeting of the Security Council, 2 March 1964. *United Nations Official Records*, S/PV.1100, para.1
73 S/PV.1100, para.7

> Recommend the creation, with the consent of the Government of Cyprus, of a United Nations peace-keeping force in Cyprus, whose composition and size would be established by the Secretary-General, in consultation with Cyprus, Greece, Turkey and the United Kingdom, and whose commander would be appointed by the Secretary-General and report to him. The Secretary-General would keep the Governments providing the force fully informed and would report periodically to the Council on its operations.[74]

At the end of his speech Bernardes expressed his 'earnest and sincere wish that the Council may see its way clear to giving its approval to the draft resolution before it'. Accepting that the various representatives to the Council might need time to consult their governments, Liu adjourned the council for twenty-four hours.

The Soviet Union requests time to consider the draft

Obviously the five non-permanent members supported the draft. In addition four of the five Permanent Members – Britain, the United States, France and China – also saw the draft resolution as being broadly acceptable. It was therefore left only to the Soviet Union to support the resolution. However, the Soviet Permanent Representative now expressed concern over the terms of the document. Despite the previous assurance given the Greek Cypriots that the draft resolution was acceptable,[75] Fedorenko's specific worry lay with the role given to the Secretary-General in the creation of the peacekeeping force.

Over the course of previous UN peacekeeping operations, the Soviet Union had become increasingly concerned about the power the Secretary-General was accumulating, at the expense, or so Moscow felt, of the Security Council. Therefore, before Fedorenko could vote on the resolution as a whole, the Soviet delegation had to cable the draft back to Moscow for guidance.[76] However, by the following day, when the Council was due to take its final decision, the Soviet Government had still not responded. Therefore, when the Council reconvened again on the afternoon of 3 March, Liu suggested another delay until the following morning. In light of this, Dean announced that he wished to make a statement:

> Of course I will bow to your wishes, Mr. President, and to the wishes of my colleagues that there should be a further adjournment, but I am bound to say that the proposal for a further adjournment does not at this moment seem to my

---

74 *The United Nations Yearbook: 1964*; p.154

75 In fact it appears that the Greek Cypriots had tried to stall on the resolution now that everyone else had agreed. In response they were told by the United States that, 'the rug market was closed.' Nicolet, *United States Policy Towards Cyprus*, p.219

76 This was not felt to be altogether surprising given the Soviet Union's known feelings about such United Nations operations. Spyros Kyprianou, interview with the author.

> delegation to be very satisfactory. I do not know quite what the reason may be, but if some of my colleagues are still waiting for their instructions, I can of course well understand that position; at some time or other we all find ourselves in the position of needing further time. But in this particular case I would urge that the Council, if it has to adjourn, should not adjourn for long. Events do not wait in Cyprus. The situation is urgent as well as important, and if it really is impossible for all concerned round this table to proceed this afternoon, I am bound, for the record, to express my Government's concern at the further delay involved.[77]

The situation in Cyprus becomes almost unbearable

Although the tabled resolution now looked almost certain to be passed, the pressures on the Truce Force were almost unbearable by this stage. Although the level of fighting had dropped since the matter went before the UN Security Council, the troops of the Joint Truce Force were by this point unable to intervene in any situations, often physically being prevented from doing so by Greek Cypriot police.[78] This inability to control the situation was mainly due to unrelenting attacks on its role appearing daily in the Greek Cypriot newspapers. Moreover, in the Greek Cypriot Communal Chamber, a representative had referred to the, 'untimely and provocative actions of the British soldiers'.[79] Similarly, a large demonstration conducted by the organisation of right-wing trade unions (SEK) in Famagusta had been attended by many carrying placards with anti-British slogans.[80] This ill feeling was further exacerbated by reports that British soldiers were carrying mail for Turkish Cypriots following the discovery of Turkish Cypriot letters in a British Forces postal bag.[81] Although all members of the Truce Force were ordered not to do it again, the Greek Cypriots nonetheless claimed that this was a clear example of London's efforts to undermine their authority and foster partition.[82] Such was the paranoia of the Greek Cypriot community towards the United Kingdom's actions by this point that there were even accusations that the President of the Turkish Communal Chamber, Rauf Denktash, was being used as a 'tool' by the British to ensure partition.[83]

It therefore came as no surprise when doubts were expressed back in Britain as to the Truce Force's operational ability to continue with the task of policing the situation. During Prime Minister's questions in the House of Commons on 3 March, it was suggested that British Army units in Cyprus were acting below strength; an accusation which refuted by the Prime Minister who drew attention to the fact that there were now 8-12,000 men on the

77 S/PV.1101, para.4

78 C.M.15 (64), 27 February 1964, *CAB 128/38*

79 *Cyprus Mail*, 1 March 1964

80 *Ibid.*

81 *The Times*, 28 February 1964

82 *Ibid.*

83 Denktash, in reply to this accusation, simply said that had the United Kingdom really wanted partition, then it would have happened. Rauf R. Denktash, interview with the Author.

island.[84] In the same session, Douglas-Home was asked whether it would have been a 'wiser' decision if the Government had put the matter to the Security Council earlier. He replied that his government,

> had to play this hand in a way which would get the agreement of the Greeks and the Turks, and we had to put a resolution to the United Nations which would not be vetoed by the Russians. That has been an extremely tricky thing to do and we should not have had a chance if we had done it earlier.'[85]

The Council meets for the final time

With the deterioration in the situation on the island now increasingly evident there was a tension surrounding the reconvening of the Security Council at ten thirty on 4 March 1964 – two days after the draft resolution was first presented. The first to speak that morning was the Permanent Representative of Soviet Union, who restated his Government's view that the Cyprus question was an internal matter best left to the Cypriots to handle.[86] However, on the question of the resolution, Fedorenko explained that,

> We consider it necessary to draw attention to those provisions in the draft resolution – we have in mind, in particular, paragraph 4 – which concern the procedure for settling matters relating to the composition, size and command of the United Nations force that it is proposed to send to Cyprus. Although the agreement of the Government of Cyprus is required for the establishment of a United Nations force in Cyprus and although the composition and size of that force are to be decided in consultation with the Governments of the so-called guaranteeing Powers – namely, the United Kingdom, Greece and Turkey – there is no escaping the fact that this procedure in practice bypasses the Security Council.
>
> Moreover, the provision in the draft resolution to the effect that the commander of the force will report to the Secretary-General, who will report periodically to the Security Council, is, of course, not adequate.[87]

The Soviet Representative therefore requested that a separate vote be taken on paragraph 4. This would allow the draft resolution to be passed in entirety but also allow the Soviet Union to register their disapproval on this particular point. However, before ending his speech the Soviet Representative landed a parting shot and soured the atmosphere by referring to the 'illegal occupation of the Presidency of the Council, and of the place

---

84 House of Commons, Official Report of Parliamentary Debates (*Hansard*), Fifth Series-Volume 690, Period 24th February-6th March, 1964, p.1131

85 *Ibid.*

86 1102nd meeting of the Security Council, 4 March 1964, *United Nations Official Records of the Security Council*, S/PV.1102, paras.2-5

87 S/PV.1102, paras.8-9

belonging to the People's Republic of China.'[88] Liu, choosing to avoid the issue for the sake of the matter at hand, passed the floor to Bernardes who, after making some comments about the structure of the resolution, passed the floor to the Secretary-General.

U Thant, obviously wishing to allay Soviet concerns, explained that it was his intention to keep the Council fully informed of a number of operational aspects pertaining to the force. In addition he made note of the fact that the United Nations force for Cyprus would, unlike UNEF or ONUC, the two previous significant UN peacekeeping operations, be set in place for a three month period, after which any extension would have to be agreed to by the Security Council. As U Thant remarked, 'In sum, although the responsibilities for the Secretary-General foreseen by the draft resolution are serious, they do not differ substantially from past experience and I have no hesitation in undertaking them.'[89]

With this concluded the President then called the votes on the resolution. The first vote was on paragraph 4 and passed by eight (8) votes to zero (0) with three abstentions – the Soviet Union, France, and Czechoslovakia. With the concern of these three officially registered, a vote could now be taken upon the entire text. The resolution was passed unanimously with no abstentions.

Following the vote, the French Representative asked to be allowed to explain his reasons for abstaining on paragraph 4. Like the Soviet Union, he said that his government was also concerned that the Secretary-General was assuming too much responsibility and that this consequently reduced the responsibilities of the Security Council.[90] Although not a personal criticism of the Secretary-General,[91] Seydoux nonetheless stressed that the French Government did not regard the responsibilities contained in the Resolution as forming a precedent.[92] The next speaker was Hajek, who, somewhat unsurprisingly, also took the stand that the Secretary-General was being given powers that rightly belonged to the Security Council.[93] In commenting on the text of the resolution as a whole Hajek noted:

> In spite of the weaknesses of the resolution, which we have had occasion to criticize in the course of conversations with its sponsors, the Czechoslovak delegation voted for it out of respect for the fact that the Cyprus delegation considers it to be acceptable and in the hope that its implementation will speedily create conditions that will facilitate the Cyprus Government's efforts to maintain and strengthen the country's independence and unity. By so doing, we have shown

---

88 S/PV.1102, para.15
89 S/PV.1102, para.24
90 S/PV.1102, para.32
91 *Ibid.* However the French Representative was known to have been harsh in his personal attitude towards U Thant. Although referring specifically to a later incident concerning the Kashmir Question, Urquhart states: 'At this time the French were also challenging the secretary general's [*sic*] authority over peacekeeping operations, and, to Bunche's annoyance, U Thant found it even more difficult to stand up properly to the French ambassador, Roger Seydoux. "U Thant," he noted, "at times chooses to give way rather than stand and fight."' Urquhart, *Ralph Bunche*, p.378
92 S/PV.1102, para.32
93 S/PV.1102, para.39

> – as we shall never fail to do – our support for the just cause of the independence, sovereignty and territorial integrity of the Republic of Cyprus and the defence and consistent application of the principles of the Charter.[94]

Liu, as President of the Council, stated the belief that all the members of the Council felt 'gratified' that the resolution of the five non-permanent members had been passed. After thanking the Cypriot Foreign Minister and the Representatives of Greece and Turkey 'for their participation and co-operation in the deliberations of the Council', the President of the Council then passed the floor to Foreign Minister Kyprianou for a final comment:

> I would like, on behalf of my Government, to express to the Council our appreciation for the understanding shown by all the members and for their sincere desire to help in solving the problems of Cyprus. Thank you, Mr. President.[95]

At this the floor returned to Liu who simply stated that, 'Since there is no further business, the meeting stands adjourned.'[96] The meeting rose at 11.40 a.m. After eleven weeks Britain was no longer directly responsible for managing the Cyprus Crisis.

---

94 S/PV.1102, para.40. Hajek in fact ended his speech by echoing Fedorenko's comment about the Presidency of the Security Council being in the hands of Liu rather than 'the only lawful representative of China'.

95 S/PV.1102, para.45

96 S/PV.1102, para.46

Conclusion

On 21 December, a few days after the Turkish Government announced that it would not accept the constitutional amendments put forward by President Makarios, fighting broke out between the Greek and Turkish Cypriot communities. Within days, it became apparent that the hostilities were more serious than at first imagined and were unlikely to subside if immediate action was not taken. In this spirit the three Guarantor Powers – Greece, Turkey and the United Kingdom – proposed the creation of a tripartite peacekeeping force to try to prevent further fighting. Once the two communities had signalled their consent to the idea, the Joint Truce Force was established. However, the difficult situation on the ground in Cyprus meant that although the Force was tripartite in name, in practice it consisted solely of British troops and the full cooperation of both the Greek and Turkish Army contingents was never realised beyond a superficial level. Despite this shortage of manpower the British troops nonetheless proved to be successful in defusing the tensions.

The efforts of the Force were also aided by high-profile support from London and the work of the Commonwealth Secretary, Duncan Sandys, who managed to negotiate a number of agreements between the two communities, including the creation of a political committee to address the key problems between the two communities. Additionally, Sandys managed to convene a conference in London – which was attended by representatives of the two communities the Government of Cyprus and the Greek and Turkish Governments – to address the substantive points of dispute. However, the London Conference soon reached deadlock as the various parties concerned quickly proved to be unwilling to reconcile their opposing views. On the one hand the Greek Cypriots sought to create a unitary state with minority safeguards. In contrast, the Turkish Cypriots demanded some form of separation between the communities based on a federal system. Neither community's option was acceptable to the other.

With the failure of the London Conference the task of the Truce Force became all the more difficult. A further rise in tension following the collapse of talks meant that what had originally been planned as a short-term intervention now looked set to become a major ongoing commitment on the part of the British Government. However the manpower demands of such an action were beyond the capabilities of London, which had military commitments in a number of other locations around the world. Attention therefore turned to other bodies that might be able to step in and carry out peacekeeping duties. However, the options available were limited to three potential candidates. In the first instance there was the United Nations. However this posed a serious chance of anti-British interference from both the Soviet Union and the Afro-Asian bloc – a factor that the United Kingdom was not prepared to risk given the strategic importance of the Sovereign Base Areas. The second alternative was to go for some form of Commonwealth force. Yet this was never explored on the basis that it would be unlikely to be able to help. The final option, thought of by Britain, but suggested by Greece, was for some form of NATO-based peacekeeping. Up until this point, international involvement in the Cyprus situation had been almost wholly limited to the Guarantor Powers. However, following Britain's approach to the Johnson Administration, the situation became subject to wider international involvement.

Following discussion between London and Washington, it was decided that a NATO-based force should be explored further. The proposal put forward by the British Government envisaged the creation of a force made up of contingents drawn from a number of NATO member states. To this extent, the plan was for a NATO-based force. The proposal was never a plan for a NATO peacekeeping force, as such. Despite this, Archbishop Makarios was opposed to any form of NATO involvement in Cyprus on the grounds that he believed that any force structured, either in whole or in part, around NATO would automatically be biased in favour of Turkey. Therefore, after several days of consideration, which was undoubtedly used to give the impression that he was opened minded about the proposal, the Archbishop formally rejected the plan. This rejection was made easier by the fact that in his opposition to such a force he was supported by the Soviet Union, which had sent a letter to the various parties concerned outlining its reason for opposing the establishment of NATO forces on the island.

This important action by the USSR effectively stalled plans to widen the force. With what at the time appeared to be a potentially dangerous East-West split now beginning to become apparent the plans for a NATO-based force were again put to Makarios. This time, however, they were presented in a more palatable manner and included references to the United Nations. However, the Archbishop was rigid in his refusal to consider the idea. By now hostility to the idea has grown across the Greek Cypriot political spectrum, even on the pro-*Enosis* right. As a result of Britain lead role in pushing the idea of a NATO-based force, hostility grew towards the Truce Force. This in turn made Britain's position as a peacekeeper increasingly untenable. Unable to replace the Force as had originally been planned, the options for the British Government, and for the western alliance as a whole, were now extremely limited. With this in mind, on 15 February the British Government took the issue of Cyprus before the United Nations Security Council.

The differences that had developed between the Greek Cypriots on the one side and the Governments of the United Kingdom and the United States on the other continued at the United Nations. The United Kingdom, although desperate to see a peacekeeping force introduced as soon as possible, nonetheless maintained a position in the Security Council that sought to have any such force created in such a way as to avoid the risk of a challenge to any of its strategic interests in general, and the Sovereign Base Areas in particular. In order to counter this, a means had to found that would minimise the role of the Soviet Union and the Afro-Asian bloc in such a way as to ensure that Moscow did not become obstructive in its approach to the matter. To this end, the British Government handled the public side of the debate by itself, leaving the United States to play a minor supporting role on the floor of the Security Council Chamber. This minimised the overt Cold War confrontation between the Superpowers, despite the fact that London and Washington maintained close contact behind the scenes. This policy was broadly successful insofar the Cold War element subsided dramatically during the phase – notwithstanding the vocal, though essentially harmless, outbursts of Ambassador Fedorenko.

On the other hand, the Greek Cypriots held that a discussion concerning the validity of the 1960 Treaties was the main reason for the debate in the Security Council. According to their thinking, if the matter on the legitimacy of intervention could be resolved in their favour, Turkey would be unable to take active military action to defend the Turkish Cypriots. Once Ankara was incapacitated, the door would then be open to having the question of violence on the island solved by the National Guard.

When it came to the debate, the Greek Cypriots, although having won a victory in taking the matter to the Security Council, were nonetheless faced with the fact that the United Kingdom maintained the procedural advantage. Furthermore, as a Permanent Member, Britain was a major force to be reckoned with inside the Chamber. While they tried to counter this influence by lobbying the other members of the Council, it quickly became clear that on the whole most of the other members were content to play the role of interlocutor and assist in finding an outcome that was broadly acceptable to all the parties. Given the fact that the Soviet role was minimised the threat to Britain by having a UN force quickly subsided and London was able to throw its support behind the establishment of a peacekeeping operation. At the same time, the Greek Cypriots found that their efforts to invalidate the treaties came to nothing as the Council showed a marked desire to avoid taking a stand on the whole question. With this question resolved, the way was paved for Resolution 186 and the creation of the United Nations Force in Cyprus (UNFICYP).

Evaluating British policy in Cyprus, 1963-64

Did London's action amount to the protection of self-interest or was there a more benign motive behind its actions? Before answering this question is must be made clear that there can be no doubt that the United Kingdom played the leading role in shaping the international responses to the crisis. Spurred primarily, though not completely, by a desire to protect its national interest in the form of the Sovereign Base Areas, Britain took responsibility for the formation of an interim peacekeeping force, and, subsequently, led both the peacemaking efforts as well as the attempts to put in place a substitute peacekeeping force. Insofar as Britain perceived a threat to the Bases, Britain's behaviour was more proactive than it might otherwise have been. Some suggested that the United Kingdom should have simply gathered together its nationals living beyond the Sovereign Base Areas and protected the perimeter. This was simply not possible. Quite apart from the fact that most of the territory of the Bases was not fenced off, abandoning the rest of the island to its fate would have almost certainly resulted in a direct Greek-Turkish confrontation. Within hours of the start of fighting Greek and Turkish contingents had left their barracks and were already supporting their Cypriot compatriots.

The problem is that throughout the period examined, London was clearly wrong in its estimation of the threat it faced from the Greek Cypriots regarding the Sovereign Base Areas. The United Kingdom saw Greek Cypriot policy throughout the period as being fundamentally designed to challenge the Treaty of Guarantee and therefore, by extension, eventually to threaten its position with regard to the Sovereign Base Areas. (Although the Bases were founded on the basis of the Treaty of Establishment, Article III of the Treaty of Guarantee held an important role in ensuring that the Republic of Cyprus would 'respect the integrity of the areas retained under United Kingdom sovereignty at the time of the establishment of the Republic of Cyprus'.)

However, this view that Makarios would try to rid Cyprus of the British bases was flawed in a number of ways. Following independence, Makarios had genuinely worked to improve the ties between Cyprus and the United Kingdom. The main forum within which this was done was the Commonwealth of Nations, which Makarios embraced warmly soon after Cypriot independence. Indeed, this move may have been a means by which Makarios could develop a separate channel of communication with the United Kingdom other than that which had been bequeathed by the Treaty of Guarantee. The Treaty, which had given the United Kingdom, Greece and Turkey a say in the affairs of the Republic of Cyprus, was simply unacceptable to many Greek Cypriots solely for the fact that it opened the door for overt Turkish interference. The ties with Greece were undoubtedly welcomed, and the ties with the United Kingdom were seen as useful – if not beneficial – given the regional strength of Turkey. In effect, the Greek Cypriots for all the ill feeling that may have occurred during the 1955-59 EOKA campaign, did want to develop their ties with the United Kingdom, and were not, with the exception of a small, particularly nationalist group, too concerned with the issue of the Bases. This is not to say that the Bases were acceptable, but that they were never an overriding issue that soured Anglo-Cypriot relations. Had this factor been fully appreciated by London, the evidence is that a suitable arrangement regarding peacekeeping could have been put in place far quicker.

Despite the fact that London was misguided in its thinking, and placed too much emphasis on the Bases, its overall approach was nonetheless benign. As will be examined later on, the Truce Force acted fully in accordance with the rules of peacekeeping and did not try to develop, let alone enforce, any particular type of political solution. In terms of the attempts to find a solution to the differences between the communities, the United Kingdom once again acted in accordance with UN principles; a fact that was recognised by U Thant, the UN Secretary-General. Furthermore, once the United States took the helm and attempted to use coercion to bring about Greek Cypriot acceptance of the NATO-based peacekeeping force proposal, Britain was noticeable by its absence. Indeed, it is worth remembering that at that stage London even declined to send a representative to accompany Ball. And once the matter was taken to the Security Council, it became clear that the overriding concern of the British Government London was to put an international force in place as soon as possible with minimal interference from the Soviet Union. Although it certainly used its influence on the other members of the Council to avoid taking a stand on the question of the Treaty of Guarantee, one can argue that this was as much in the best interests of the Greek Cypriots as it was of Britain, the United States, and the whole of NATO. In conclusion, one can say that British policy was essentially incorrect in its underlying premise, but that, on the whole, it was not based on neo-colonialism or hostility but was simply structured on a multiplicity of national and international requirements and interests: the need to protect the Bases, the need to restore peace and stability to the island and the need to ensure the stability of the surrounding region.

The roles of Greece and Turkey

In the case of the roles played by Greece and Turkey, some very interesting facts are readily apparent. It should be remembered that beyond the desire to protect its national interests, the other reason why Britain created the Truce Force was to avert the prospect of a Greek-Turkish conflict over Cyprus. In reality, such a prospect was highly unlikely. Both Greece and Turkey acted with remarkable restraint throughout the crisis. In the case of Greece, domestic political instability had resulted in the formation of caretaker government under John Paraskevopoulos, which was, by its very nature, cautious and technocratic. However, Greece was never likely to stage a unilateral first strike intervention either. By the time of the election of a new government led by George Papandreou, in mid-February, when there was a rise in rhetoric against Turkey, the question of peacekeeping had already been moved to the United Nations, thus minimising the problem of the new government's overtly nationalistic rhetoric.

Like Greece, Turkey, which undoubtedly had more to play for in Cyprus, displayed a willingness to refrain from intervening in order to allow peace-making and peacekeeping efforts by first the United Kingdom, and then by the United Kingdom and the United States. Despite its numerous threats to intervene as well as its periodic military mobilisations, Turkey nonetheless showed a commendable degree of restraint at the time Indeed, such was the willingness of the Turkish Government to work in conjunction with the United Kingdom and the United States that on two separate, but vitally important, occasions it actually avoided taking a stand in favour of the Turkish Cypriot community. The first time was in London when Foreign Minister Erkin persuaded the Turkish Cypriot delegation to remain despite the fact that the Greek Cypriots had managed to have two delegations recognised – one as the Greek Cypriot community and the other as the Government of the Republic of Cyprus, from which the Turkish Cypriots were excluded. The second period was when Turkey sided with the United Kingdom and the United States and persuaded the Turkish Cypriots to accept the proposed terms of Resolution 186. These two incidents perhaps represent the most vital periods in securing for the Greek Cypriots recognition of their position as the legal Government of the Republic of Cyprus. One may contest the degree to which any Turkish opposition to these issues may have actually affected any outcome, but one cannot contest the fact that Turkey did, nonetheless, play a significant part in the events that led to the eventual alienation of the Turkish Cypriot community from the apparatus of the Government of Cyprus that resulted from the *de facto*, if not *de jure*, recognition of the Greek Cypriot leadership as the rightful holders of that title. If the aim of the United Kingdom and the United States was to avoid a Greco-Turkish conflict in the Eastern Mediterranean, the actions of both Greece and Turkey throughout the greater part of the period reviewed were to be commended.

The role of the United States

The role of the United States also provides some fascinating conclusions. Although the United States acted in conjunction, though very cautiously, with the Guarantors in the initial phase of the crisis it was not immediately in favour of becoming overtly involved. Instead, the new US administration, formed by Lyndon Johnson after the assassination of John F. Kennedy the previous month, was seemingly wary of overextending the US role in the crisis so early in its term. It therefore chose to exert diplomatic pressure on Greece and Turkey, rather than target the Cypriot communities. This was, on the face of it a stabilising move as it maintained the importance of the Guarantor Alliance as the directly interested parties to the crisis, and thus prevented the undesirable internationalisation of the situation. The mistake made by the United Kingdom with regard to the United States was that it played too heavily upon the dangers of NATO instability if such Guarantor cohesion broke down. Yet, despite the essentially calm way in which both Greece and Turkey had handled the Cyprus crisis, the United Kingdom necessarily had to highlight the dangers of a potential Greek-Turkish split in order to develop the interest of the United States in the situation. It could not present a plan to the United States that asked for its involvement in Cyprus simply because it could no longer bear the burden alone – a move that had already been done once at the end of the Second World War. When the United Kingdom did try that tactic, in the period before the London Conference, the US Administration asked the British Government to consider looking elsewhere, for example to the Commonwealth. However, this option had already been discounted on the, arguably weak, basis that the Commonwealth would not be able to meet the burden. Therefore in order to bring the United States into the situation as a credible actor, it would have to be presented with a situation serious enough to warrant its involvement. The threat to NATO stability was such a reason.

Once the United States had considered and accepted this danger, it took up the cause with ill-concealed gusto. Indeed, its diplomatic actions soon left the United Kingdom, for the most part, as a secondary actor in the process – a position that the British Government undoubtedly favoured. The burden of the Truce Force was taking enough of its energies and political resources, and to be relieved of the extra burden of trying to maintain the overall cooperation of the Guarantor Powers in the face of Makarios's internationalisation of the issue was not something to be mourned. Yet such involvement by the United States was necessarily fraught with danger. Cyprus was a member of the Non-Aligned Movement and not of NATO, and therefore to pressure the Cypriots to accept a NATO-based option could easily have been interpreted as an example of NATO expansionism. There was no way in which the situation could be regarded as one of containment at this point as the Soviet Union had taken only the slightest of interest in the conflict. By not considering the strength of Greek Cypriot opposition to the NATO-based plan, the United States and the United Kingdom allowed Makarios to internationalise the matter. With NATO involvement, Makarios could encourage the Soviet Union to take a more robust role in the problem. However, once the matter had been successfully moved to the Security Council, the United States took a step back and allowed Britain to play the lead role, with only limited interference from that point onwards.

The role of the Soviet Union

This brings us to the role of the Soviet Union. First and foremost, one can argue that Moscow conducted its policy towards the island in absolute accordance with its overall international policies at the time. In the first stage of the crisis, when Greece, Turkey and the United Kingdom had been involved, the Soviet Administration remained fairly disengaged. The reason for this aloofness is perhaps best explained by the fact that the Soviet Union simply interpreted the events in Cyprus to be wholly within the Western realm, and therefore to become involved would risk a direct confrontation with the United States. This impression of western involvement could only have been confirmed by the fact that Makarios had actually sanctioned the tripartite intervention by the Guarantor Powers. This may explain why the Soviet Union remained quiet even when the issue of a Turkish threat to Cyprus came up in the first Security Council session in December 1963. (However, if one wanted to find a justification for the Soviet Union's lack of action at this point, one could argue that the Soviet Union was aware of the delicate nature of the Greek Cypriots position, but deliberately remained quiet in order not to upset the process of the withdrawal of US missiles from Turkey that had secretly been reached during the Cuban Missile Crisis.)

However, something happened to change this. Denktash's allegations that Makarios encouraged the Soviet Union to become involved in Cyprus has never been truly answered – and probably never will with complete certainty. The opposing views on the issue do not fall along communal lines. Although most Turkish Cypriots assert that Makarios approached the Soviet Union,[1] there are those who see it in terms of each approaching the other at the same time.[2] In the Greek Cypriot community, opinion is even more divided. For example, one of the leading communist figures on the island at the time, Andreas Ziartides, stated that he believed that Makarios went to the Soviet Union;[3] a view supported by many other Greek Cypriots.[4] However, there are those who disagree, including Vassos

1 Rauf R. Denktash and Necati Ertekun, interviews with the author.
2 Osman Orek and Zaim Necatigil, interviews with the author.
3 Andreas Ziartides, interview with the author.
4 Among the more prominent writers on Cyprus who have supported this view see Coufoudakis, 'United States Foreign Policy and the Cyprus Question: A Case Study in Cold War Diplomacy' in Attalides (ed.),

Lyssarides, who was a close advisor to the Archbishop and was a leading supporter of non-alignment .[5] Yet again, there are those who see the diplomatic process as being two-way in nature.[6]

The emphasis must however remain on the fact that Makarios encouraged the Soviet Union, rather than the argument that the Soviet Union deliberately pressured Makarios. Further evidence for this was the fact that the *TASS* statement had noted that 'the Government of Cyprus had informed the Soviet Government' that there was now 'a serious danger of aggression against Cyprus.'[7] This fear on the part of the Greek Cypriots could well have been expressed at what was described as a 'long meeting' between the acting-Cypriot Foreign Minister Araouzos and the Soviet Ambassador on 27 January.[8] In addition the fact that the Soviet Union had not become involved earlier was directly attributed by some press editorials to the fact that the Greek Cypriots had not approached it. For example *Eleftheria* stated, 'it is not the fault of the Soviet Union if its representations against foreign intervention in Cyprus have been a little late. The fault lies with the Cyprus Government, which has fallen into the trap of the London Conference by giving faith to promises which have proven false.'[9]

In terms of the lack of Soviet interest until this point one can point to the fact Moscow did not want to become too engaged with the United States in the aftermath of the Cuban Missile Crisis, a little over a year earlier. However, its decision to become involved does fit neatly with Moscow's opportunistic foreign policy that had been followed by the Soviet Union since 1955, and which seems to have increased in the aftermath of Cuba. In any case, the Cyprus situation provided the elements that raised Moscow's interest in becoming involved:[10]

Cyprus Reviewed, p.112. Joseph, 'The UN as an Instrument of National Policy: The Case of Cyprus', p.49. Perhaps the most important comment on the issue comes from the former Greek Consul-General in Cyprus during the EOKA years who goes as far as to identify when the approach was made: 'On 27 January 1964 the Archbishop - bearing in mind that Greece has very limited possibilities of acting effectively not only for bringing the situation under control but also for warding off worse developments - makes a serious mistake. The Acting Minister of Foreign Affairs in Cyprus, Araouzos, seeks from the Ambassador of the USSR in Cyprus the assistance of Moscow.' See Vlachos, *Deka Chronia Kypriakou.* An English translation is cited in Reddaway, *Burdened With Cyprus. The British Connection*, p.222

5 Vassos Lyssarides, during an interview with the author, stated that he, "did not believe that Makarios would approach the Soviet Union." Tassos Papadopoulos, in an interview with the author stated that, "Makarios was not a communist...and would not have approached the Soviet Union as a Castro."

6 Christodoulos Veniamin, during an interview with the author noted that, "immediately after the clashes Makarios sent diplomatic missions everywhere, including the Soviet Union". Chris Economides stated that it is difficult to say definitively whether Makarios approached the Soviet Union, or the Soviet Union approached Makarios. Chris Economides, interview with the author.

7 *Reuters*, 30 January 1964

8 *Cyprus Mail*, 28 January 1964

9 *Eleftheria*, 1 February 1964

10 These ideas are in line with the thinking of Thomas Adams, a former US State Department official who has been a commentator on communism in Cyprus for over thirty years (see Bibliography for examples). Dr. Thomas Adams, personal interview with the author. Andreas Ziartides, a member of AKEL's politburo at the time, in an interview with the author, stated that these three points were, "in direct relation to the Soviet Union's Cold War policy." Osman Orek concurred with this assessment, interview with the author.

1. An increase in NATO's field of operation beyond its more traditionally defined area to incorporate a Non-Aligned Movement member state.
2. A chance to embarrass the NATO alliance on the World stage.
3. Ensuring that actions on such issues should, wherever possible, be decided at the United Nations Security Council, where the Soviet Union could have a say in the outcome. (This explains the letter sent by the Soviet Union to U Thant, criticising the way in which the Secretary General had acted with clear authorisation from the Council.)

Had it not been for the fact that Makarios approached the Soviet Union when the issue of NATO-based peacekeeping arose, it is fair to argue that Moscow would [probably have remained quiet on the issue. In the event, by approaching the already interested Soviet Union with the NATO threat posed against the island, which was a member of the Non-Aligned Movement, the Archbishop was able to encourage the typical opportunistic behaviour that had so often characterised Soviet foreign policy. For both Makarios and the Soviet Union, the actions of the United Kingdom and the United States with regard to Cyprus meant that the Greek Cypriots were now engaged in a form of national liberation movement to exert the right to express its own sovereignty in the face of NATO pressure. And yet after it was approached, Moscow reacted perhaps a little more forcefully – within the bounds of opportunistic behaviour – than many could have expected. The Khrushchev Letter of 7 February was undoubtedly hard-hitting in its tone; the question is whether it was hard-hitting in substance? On the basis of the resulting events it appears that it did have some effect. However, this effect may have had as much, if not more, to do with internal NATO problems as with Khrushchev's text. In any case, even if one were to ascribe a great deal of significance to the Soviet letter it did not stop the United States from pursuing the idea of a NATO-based peace-keeping force, although one could argue that it may have ensured that the United States could not force any peace-keeping option upon the Greek Cypriots. Thereafter, while supporting the position of the Greek Cypriots, the Soviets became far more muted in their activities and, during the Security Council debates, shifted its attention more towards the operational matters of peacekeeping. Thus while, Moscow did play an important role, at an important time, it is possible to say that its overall impact on the development of the situation at the time was rather limited in comparison to the extent that many expected its role would be.

The role of the Non-Aligned Movement

One element of the international community at that time that is notably missing is the Non-Aligned Movement NAM). Before analysing the absence of the NAM from this story, it is worth mentioning a few details about the Movement as it was by 1964. First, and foremost, it must be remembered that the Non-Aligned Movement was not formalised in the way that both NATO and the Warsaw Treaty Organisation were; indeed, the NAM had only had one full conference by the time of Cyprus – the meeting in Belgrade in 1961. Instead, it is best viewed as a grouping of states that held a common viewpoint on a number of issues and, as such, felt that issues arising in international politics should be judged not by the criteria of the Superpowers but instead should be appraised on the merits of the individual case.

In any case, it is interesting to note that throughout the period covered the Non-Aligned Movement – as a collective association of states – had remained remarkably quiet on the subject of Cyprus; a fellow member. Although there had been a degree of interest shown by certain individual members of the Movement – including Yugoslavia which, from the evidence available, had alone called the active support of the Movement as a whole for Cyprus as an 'urgent necessity'[11] – there had been little overt action taken by the other member states to support Cyprus directly. Indeed, apart from Tito, the few members who did state an opinion did tend to be the Arab states, of which Egypt, which under the leadership of Colonel Nasser, who was close to Makarios, was the most prominent.[12] However, their statements seemed to show more concern about the possibility that the Cyprus situation being orchestrated by the West as a means to provide a staging point for future support of Israel,[13] than about the way in which the Greek Cypriots were being pressured by Britain and the United States. One cannot be entirely sure as to why this might have been the case. Such a course of action on the part of the Arab states may possibly – though this cannot be proved with any certainty – have been as a result of a dilemma faced by the states: although Makarios had a prominent position within the NAM, the minority group in the conflict were Moslem, albeit Turkish. Of course, Morocco also raised the issue on the floor of the Security Council, but this was hardly a strong statement of support.

There is also an argument that the lack of NAM involvement was because the Greek Cypriots did not directly ask for the support of the Movement. Although this may sound an easy way out of trying to address this problem there are several good reasons why this may have been the case. In the first instance, the Greek Cypriots had apparently shown a marked disdain for the idea of some form of African involvement in a potential peacekeeping force organised by the Commonwealth. This seems to signify a degree of xenophobia with regard to potential non-white involvement in Cyprus. While the NAM may have been a good forum by which to participate in the general airing of third world views on a number of important developmental issues, there was not, perhaps, a marked interest at this stage on the part of the Greek Cypriots to have the organisation involved in the affairs of Cyprus.

Secondly, there was no reason for the Greek Cypriots to approach the NAM and that by the time they could have asked for specific NAM involvement the issue had become a far too partisan a Cold War issue. In the initial phase of the crisis when the matter was held within the sphere of the Guarantor Powers, events seemed to be progressing in such a way that the need overtly to internationalise the problem beyond the general forum of the United Nations, was not deemed necessary. However, when the matter of the force made up of contingents from NATO member states arose, the matter immediately became of direct concern to the Soviet Union; this therefore by-passed the NAM as an option. In any case, it

11 *Cyprus Mail*, 16 February 1964
12 Vassos Lyssarides, interview with the author.
13 *The Times*, 3 February 1964

appears as though the general feeling was that the Movement would not have been able to provide as effective a means of countering the NATO 'threat' as the Soviet Union.

An evaluation of the Joint Truce Force

One aspect of this story that has been truly forgotten in history is the work of the Joint Truce Force during the months it took to finally establish an alternative peacekeeping force. In the traditional theory of peacekeeping one judges whether an operation is actually a peacekeeping action according to three criteria: namely that the force is there with the consent of the host state, that it follows the principle of non-enforcement and that it is seen to be impartial in the conduct of its operation.[14]

The Joint Truce Force clearly met the two first conditions with little difficulty. From the start the Force was in Cyprus with the consent of both the communities of Cyprus. Indeed, it is worth noting that Britain, Greece and Turkey deliberately chose to avoid taking conjoint action under the provisions of the Treaty of Guarantee and instead opted for a mission undertaken with the consent of the parties. Moreover, while there were a number of groups that became increasingly opposed to the Truce Force over the course of its operation, it was never openly challenged by either President Makarios or Vice-President Kuchuk. On the second point, regarding non-enforcement, we can say that although there was an incident when shots were fired over the heads of demonstrators, the Force conducted its operation in a non-coercive manner, in spirit as well as action, during the whole period under review. Evidence supporting the view that the intention of the Force was never intended to develop an enforcement policy can perhaps be drawn from the fact that although the units sent to Cyprus were diverse and included artillery units, in all cases the heavy guns attached to these units were left behind in the United Kingdom.

The final point that needs to be addressed is that of the impartiality of the Force. There have been a number of criticisms made regarding the alleged bias of the Truce Force towards one or other community during the Cyprus Crisis. However, and importantly, these have come from both sides of the Green Line, and, in the course of reviewing the actions of the Force, there seems to be little to merit such accusations. In the first instance, the troops serving with the Truce Force were targeted by both the Greek and Turkish Cypriot militias, rather than by just one or other of the factions. Secondly, the fact that the Force came between the two must not be seen as evidence that they were attempting to protect the Turkish Cypriots who were often the weaker party. Peacekeeping involves interposition,

14 The United Nations defines peacekeeping as, 'an operation involving military personnel, but without enforcement powers, undertaken by the United Nations to help maintain or restore international peace and security in areas of conflict. These operations are voluntary and are based on consent and cooperation. While they involve the use of military personnel, they achieve their objectives not by the force of arms, thus contrasting them with 'enforcement action of the United Nations under Article 42.' *The Blue Helmets*, 2nd Edition, p.90. For a discussion of the applicability of non-UN peacekeeping see Ker-Lindsay, *The Origins of the United Nations Force in Cyprus*, pp.3-5

and to argue that this action is biased is to argue that all peacekeeping forces must sit to one side for fear of being identified as being partial to the weaker side. On the issue of impartiality, it would therefore seem fair to say that the Force was impartial. It was an unfortunate outcome of the situation that, at one point or another, both communities argued that the Force's impartiality was intended to help the other side.

In spite of this assessment, there are likely to be those within the Greek Cypriot community who will always maintain that the political guidance given to the Joint Truce Force was designed to favour the Turkish Cypriots and therefore to assist in securing the partition of the island. The available evidence does not seem to support this argument. Instead, during the course of the period under review, the operational orders given in the field remained true to the aim of ensuring that a peace was maintained between the fighting factions rather than follow a particular political agenda. If impartiality means that a peacekeeping force displays no obvious bias towards any particular conflicting party, but that it displays a clear partiality towards the implementation of its mandate, even if a party to the conflict might interpret this negatively, then the Truce Force was indeed impartial.

However, there are two further reasons for judging the Truce Force as a peacekeeping entity. In the first case the various documents released by the British Government often refer to, if not emphasise, the fact that the Truce Force was peacekeeping, and, correspondingly, never cite it as being a coercive undertaking. In the second instance, we can point to the fact that very often peacekeeping forces are detailed to develop a humanitarian role. Again there were clear examples of cases where the Force carried out humanitarian work and thus met the criteria for being assessed as a peacekeeper.

Despite these arguments, the fact remains that for many the term 'peacekeeping' does not sit comfortably when applied to the Joint Truce Force. What seems to be the enduring image in the minds the Greek Cypriots was that the Force was undeniably British in nature. Even though people from both communities who remember the period agree that it fulfilled an important role in calming inter-communal tensions at the time, the fact is that the Force was always viewed in a slightly suspicious way by a large number of Greek Cypriots. This appears to devolve from the fact that the soldiers of the Force were wearing the uniform of the British Army which had, less than four years earlier, been the sworn enemy of most of the majority Greek Cypriot population. And although it seems to be the case that most of those interviewed were able to differentiate clearly between the British Army as an entity trying to keep the peace in 1963-64 from the British Army which was the tool by which the United Kingdom attempted to retain its colonial position in Cyprus in 1955-59, the temptation to accuse the Truce Force of following a neo-colonial enterprise was too much to resist for elements in the Greek Cypriot community when events, unrelated to the operational actions of the Truce Force, went against them. In the final analysis, the simple fact of the matter is that although the Joint Truce Force was an undeniable force for good in those days, and that it followed the tenets of peacekeeping, it was always likely to have been seen as the army of the former colonial power and treated accordingly.

Appendix A: UN Resolution 186 (1964)

The Security Council,

Noting that the present situation with regard to Cyprus is likely to threaten international peace and security and may further deteriorate unless additional measures are promptly taken to maintain peace and to seek out a durable solution,

Considering the positions taken by the parties in relation to the Treaties signed at Nicosia on 16 August 1960,

Having in mind the relevant provisions of the Charter of the United Nations and its Article 2, paragraph 4, which reads: 'All members shall refrain in their international relations from the threat or use of force against the territorial integrity or political independence of any State, or in any other manner inconsistent with the purposes of the United Nations',

1. Calls upon all Member States, in conformity with their obligations under the Charter of the United Nations, to refrain from any action or threat of action to worsen the situation in the sovereign Republic of Cyprus, or to endanger international peace;

2. Asks the Government of Cyprus, which has the responsibility for the maintenance and restoration of law and order, to take all additional measures necessary to stop violence and bloodshed in Cyprus;

3. Calls upon the communities in Cyprus and their leaders to act with the utmost restraint;

4. Recommends the creation, with the consent of the Government of Cyprus, of a United Nations Peace-Keeping Force in Cyprus. The composition and size of the Force shall be established by the Secretary-General, in consultation with the Governments of Cyprus, Greece, Turkey, and the United Kingdom. The commander of the Force shall be appointed by the Secretary-General and report to him. The Secretary-General, who shall keep the Governments providing the Force fully informed, shall report periodically to the Security Council on its operation;

5. Recommends that the function of the Force should be in the interest of preserving international peace and security, to use its best efforts to prevent a recurrence of fighting and, as necessary, to contribute to the maintenance and restoration of law and order and a return to normal conditions;

6. Recommends that the stationing of the Force shall be for a period of three months, all costs pertaining to it being met, in a manner to be agreed upon by them, by the Governments providing the contingents and by the Government of Cyprus. The Secretary-General may also accept voluntary contributions for the purpose;

7. Recommends further that the Secretary-General designate, in agreement with the Government of Cyprus and the Governments of Greece, Turkey and United Kingdom a mediator who shall use his best endeavours with the representatives of the communities and also with the aforesaid four Governments, for the purpose of promoting a peaceful solution and an agreed settlement of the problem confronting Cyprus, in accordance with the Charter of the United Nations, having in mind the well- being of the people as a whole and the preservation of international peace and security. The mediator shall report periodically to the Secretary-General on his efforts;

8. Requests the Secretary-General to provide, from funds of the United Nations, as appropriate, for the remuneration and expenses of the mediator and his staff.

Appendix B: The Khrushchev Letter and Replies

I. The Text of the Letter from Chairman Khrushchev (7 February 1964)

I consider it necessary to address you in the name of the Soviet Government in connection with the fact that of late the situation around the Republic of Cyprus is becoming increasingly heated, creating a danger of serious international complications in the area of the Mediterranean Sea. The causes of the tension which has arisen are well known: the disagreements between the two communities in Cyprus - the Greeks, who constitute the majority of the population, and the Turks - have long been heated from outside, and they are being used as a pretext for unconcealed intervention in the internal affairs of the Republic of Cyprus - a sovereign, independent State and a member of the United Nation Organisation.

Some Powers, trampling on the principles of the Charter of the United Nations and the universally accepted norms of International Law, are now trying to impose on the people and Government of Cyprus a solution favourable to these Powers of problems which affect only Cypriots, and furthermore they are conveying the impression that the solution of these internal problems can be brought to Cyprus only on foreign bayonets. In this connection variants of "solutions" are being discussed - for example, the despatch to Cyprus of NATO troops or of troops from individual NATO countries, although basically all these variants have one aim - the factual occupation by the armed forces of NATO of the Republic of Cyprus, which follows a policy of non-adherence to military blocs. In other words, it is a question of a gross infringement of the sovereignty, independence and freedom of the Republic of Cyprus, of an attempt to place this small neutral State under the military control of NATO.

In the minds of all those who are interested in the preservation of peace, in ensuring for any States-large or small, strong or weak-the possibility of building their national life in accordance with their own interests and aspirations, there arises the question: if the sovereignty of States is not an empty phrase written in the United Nations Charter, if the right to freedom and independence is really a sacred right of all peoples, of all States, then why do they wish to exclude the Republic of Cyprus from the number of those who are allowed to enjoy the benefits of sovereignty and to build their own national life without intervention from outside? Do they not think that sovereignty is the right of only the strong, and that genuine independence is the privilege only of those who dispose of powerful armed forces? Do they not thus consider that small States, such as the Republic of Cyprus, which possesses neither atomic weapons nor numerous armed forces, constitute States of some other sort, to the sovereignty and rights of which consideration need not be paid?

Such views, if the Governments of Great Powers, especially the permanent members of the Security Council, were guided by them, could constitute a serious danger for universal peace, and could become a source of international complications, fraught with grave consequences for the peoples.

Sometimes in justification of the plans for the dispatch of NATO troops to Cyprus, the point of view is expressed that the Cypriots are not able to settle their own internal problems on their own, that they cannot reach agreement on how the Greek and Turkish communities should live together within the framework of a single State. But who can better know whether the Cypriots can overcome their internal difficulties independently without any intervention from abroad than the Cypriots themselves, who, under the leadership of their Government and of President Makarios, are manfully and firmly defending the sovereignty of their Republic, defending their national independence, their rights? Is there really a wish to make anyone believe that it is easier to deal with the internal problems of Cyprus in the capitals of other countries? And it is no secret that in NATO circles discussion is proceeding on the question whether to send to Cyprus as part of the so-called "NATO forces" soldiers of the German Bundeswehr, though in these regions memories have by no means completely faded of the steel helmets of the soldiers of the Wehrmacht, which during the years of the Second World war brought destruction and death to the area of the Mediterranean Sea.

We are convinced that the Cypriots are fully able to deal with their internal affairs themselves, as the Government of the Republic of Cyprus has repeatedly stated, and to find for the problems which confront them solutions which will accord in the highest degree with their national interests. But we are prepared to admit that other States may have a different approach to this question, and in their evaluation the situation may be such that the people of Cyprus really needs help in overcoming its internal difficulties. But even if that were the case, at the utmost it could only be a question of giving the Cypriots good advice if they asked for it, and in no case of intervention in their internal affairs.

And if one is to speak of the review of the Cyprus question in an international forum, do there not exist between all States agreements, embodied in the United Nations Charter, laying down where and in which international organs such questions should be considered and how it is appropriate to do this without violating the Sovereignty of States? Yet at present everything is being done to prevent the discussion of the Cyprus question in the Security Council, on whose agenda it was placed at the request of the Government of Cyprus. And this is being done in spite of the fact that the Security Council is precisely the organ charged under the Charter of the United Nations with ensuring international peace and security.

Everything conceivable is being done at present in order to prevent the further consideration of the Cyprus question in the Security Council. The Government of Cyprus is being made the object of persuasion, it is being subjected to pressure. It is being threatened, military demonstrations are being conducted near the coasts of Cyprus, the flag of naval blockade is being waved, and meanwhile efforts of all kinds are being made to prevent a new appeal by the Government of Cyprus to the Security Council.

From all this it is evident that preference is being given to the consideration of the Cyprus question at closed conferences, where, having replaced the United Nations Charter by arbitrary methods, people are counting on breaking the resistance of a small State, the Republic of Cyprus, by means of pressure from outside.

Taking into account all the circumstances which have arisen in connection with plans for the organisation of military intervention against the Republic of Cyprus, I should like to state that the Soviet Government condemns such plans, just as it condemns in general the use of such methods in the practice of international relations. The Soviet Government appeals to all States concerned, and first to all the permanent members of the Security Council who bear a responsibility for the maintenance of international peace and security, including the United States and Great Britain, to show restraint, to make a realistic and all-round assessment of all the consequences to which a military invasion of Cyprus could lead, to respect the sovereignty and independence of the Republic of Cyprus.

In making this appeal, which is dictated by care for the preservation and consolidation of peace and for ensuring the rights of peoples, I also start from the premise that the Soviet Union, although it is not immediately adjacent to the republic of Cyprus, cannot remain indifferent to the situation which is developing in the area of the Eastern

Mediterranean, an area which is not so far removed from the Southern frontiers of the USSR, especially if account is taken of how the concept of distance has changed in our time.

I think that abstention from any plans which might make more acute the situation in the area of the Eastern Mediterranean and infringe the legitimate rights of the people of Cyprus to freedom and independence would be in accordance not only with the common interests of the Cypriots but with our interests. The leaders of the Great Powers have repeatedly stated that they are aiming at the reduction of international tension, irrespective of whether this concerns Central Europe, the Mediterranean or any other area. If this is so, then it seems to me that the whole of their weight, the whole international authority and influence of the leading Statesmen of the Soviet Union, the United States of America, Great Britain, France and also of the States which are neighbours of Cyprus-Turkey and Greece-should now be used in order not to permit any further heating of the situation around Cyprus, in order to extinguish the passions which are being heated from abroad, and which have already exercised such a negative influence on the situation, and thereby to contribute to the consolidation of peace in this important area. I should like, Mr. Prime Minister, to express the hope that your Government will correctly understand the motives by which the Soviet Government is guided in again raising its voice in defence of the just cause of the Republic of Cyprus and that it will take due account of the considerations set out in the present communication.

House of Commons, Official Report of Parliamentary Debates (HANSARD), Fifth Series-Volume 689, Comprising the Period 10th-21st February, 1964, (London: Her Majesty's Stationery Office) pp.108-111 (Written Answers)

II. Text of the Reply from Prime Minister Paraskevopoulos of Greece (11 February 1964)

I wish to thank you for your message of 7th instant regarding the developments in the question of Cyprus. The position of the Greek Government on this question is known, as well as its dedication to a policy of insuring the fundamental rights of the Cypriots and preserving the independence and territorial integrity of the State of Cyprus. At the present stage and following the occurrence of communal strife our efforts are aimed at the pacification of the island, not through intervention, but through the granting of the international support and assistance requested for the above purpose by the Government of Cyprus.

'Message dated 11 February 1964 from the Prime Minister of Greece to the Chairman of the Council of Ministers of the Union of Soviet Socialist Republics concerning the question of Cyprus' (Unofficial translation). Contained in 'Letter dated 15 February from the Representative of Greece to the Secretary-General', United Nations Security Council Document, S/5549

III. Text of the Reply from President Johnson of the United States (4 March 1964)

I have carefully studied the letter you sent to me on February 7 concerning the situation in Cyprus, and I can only conclude that, whatever may have been the motivations of the Soviet government, your message was based upon a seriously mistaken appreciation both of the situation in Cyprus, and of the United States in agreeing to lend its assistance in improving that situation. The United States has been cooperating with the Governments concerned, including the Government of the Republic of Cyprus, for one purpose alone, that of assisting the Cypriots to restore a peaceful situation in Cyprus. I will, however, agree fully, Mr. Chairman, with one though that you expressed in your letter. It is certainly true that avoiding the aggravation of the situation in the Eastern Mediterranean is in the general interests of all of us. We should all strive not to inflame passions from without. I can assure you that this is the firm intention of my Government, and I sincerely hope, Mr. Chairman, that it is also that of your Government.

Washington to FO, No.883, 4 March 1964, FO 371/174747

IV. Text of the Reply from Prime Minister Inonu of Turkey (24 February 1964)

I have received and studied the message dated February 7 which you sent via the Turkish Ambassador in Moscow. In spite of the comprehensive and open information given to the USSR by the Turkish Ministry of Foreign Affairs in its note dated January 29 about the nature of the Cyprus problem, the international Agreements which bear the signature of the Republic of Cyprus, the terrible events of the last months and Turkey's extremely patient and moderate behaviour based on the Agreements, I learn with astonishment and grief that your message dated February 7, without taking into account all these facts and the bloody assaults which are still continuing in Cyprus, makes several attacks on Turkey.

Mr. President, Despite the cease-fire agreement which the Greek Cypriots signed on December 29, 1963, armed attacks on Turkish Cypriots are continuing. Almost every day, Greek police in official uniform and EOKA bandits are attacking Turkish villages in the Turkish sectors of towns and, with no distinction for age or sex, are opening fire, burning Turkish houses and later destroying them. At present, over 15 thousand Turkish Cypriots who have survived Greek attacks have left their homes, fields and flocks and squeezed themselves into the various Turkish Sectors. These refugees are living in tents, schools and cafés during the winter months under very hard material conditions and under the threat of fresh attack. On February 13, Greek police and civilians held the Turkish Sector of Limassol under shell, bazooka and heavy machine-gun fire for 48 hours. Up to now, it has been proved that Turks in Limassol have been killed and wounded in large numbers. Continuous representations to the responsible Greek Cypriot administration in order to put an end to the bloodshed and guarantee security of life and property have unfortunately produced no result. Every day several Turks are killed and their houses destroyed.

The Government of the USSR is undoubtedly aware of the terrible events which are taking place before everyone's eyes and which have been publicised by the world press and television. It is seriously hard to understand why there is not the slightest hint, in your message, of the systematic attacks which are being made on innocent and defenceless people.

Mr. President, There is no connection between the international force, whose despatch to Cyprus is being contemplated, and the aims and intentions which you mention in your message. The duty of the international force consists of guaranteeing complete security of life, property and personal liberty for all, of putting an end to today's terrorism and of creating the possibility of searching for a solution to the Cyprus problem for all the interested parties in a calm atmosphere.

It is a fact that Turkey has always carried out its relations with Cyprus scrupulously and in a manner conforming to the principles of existing contracts. It will be remembered that these contracts consist of the Agreements which came into existence after long and detailed negotiations to the mutual satisfaction of Turkey, Britain, Greece and the Turkish and Greek Cypriot communities, in accordance with a motion, concerning the means of solving the Cyprus problem between the interested parties, which was proposed after many difficult discussions in the United Nations and accepted unanimously by the 13th General Assembly.

Among other things, these Agreements proposed and recognized reciprocal rights and obligations for both Greek and Turkish communities in the Island, and at the same time brought into existence the Republic of Cyprus to respect these principles and to guarantee them in a proper manner.

After the formation of the Republic of Cyprus within the framework of these Agreements, when its request for membership of the United Nations was being discussed, both in the Security Council and in the General Assembly, the internal Constitution and the special powers were submitted to the attention of the United Nations and this request for membership was accepted unanimously.

Respect for international law and existing agreements and the peaceful solution of international disputes are the unchanging principles of Turkish foreign policy and will continue to be so.

This letter was originally submitted to the British Embassy in Ankara in Turkish. The Turkish Government apologised 'for the fact that it was not accompanied by a translation but explained that as the Russians had sent their note to them in Russian without even an unofficial translation, they had acted similarly and merely sent their note in Turkish.' FO 371/174748

Bibliography

Adams, Thomas W. *US Army Area Handbook for Cyprus* (Washington: US Government Printing Office, 1964)

Adams, Thomas W. *AKEL. The Communist Party of Cyprus* (Stanford, California: Hoover Institution Press, 1971)

Adams, Thomas W. and Alvin J. Cottrell. *Cyprus. Between East and West* Studies in International Affairs, Number 7, (Baltimore: The Johns Hopkins Press, 1968)

Alastos, Doros. *Cyprus in History* (London: Zeno Publishers, 1955)

Anderson, David M. "Policing and Communal Conflict: The Cyprus Emergency, 1954-60" *The Journal of Imperial and Commonwealth History*, Volume XXI, Number 3, September 1993

Attalides, Michael A. (ed.) *Cyprus Reviewed.* (Nicosia: The Jus Cypri Association, 1976)

Bahceli, Tozun. *Greek-Turkish Relations since 1955* (London: Westview Press, 1990)

Ball, George. *The Past Has Another Pattern. Memoirs* (London: WW Norton & Company, 1982)

Birgisson, Karl. "United Nations Peacekeeping Force in Cyprus'" in William J. Durch (ed.) *The Evolution of UN Peacekeeping. Case Studies and Comparative Analysis* (London: Macmillan, 1993)

Bitsios, Dimitri S. *Cyprus. The Vulnerable Republic* (Thessaloniki: Institute for Balkan Studies, 1975)

Bourantonis, Dimitris and Marios Evriviades (eds.) *A United Nations for the Twenty-First Century. Peace Security and Development* (London: Kluwer Law International, 1996)

Carver, Michael (Field Marshal Lord) *Out of Step. The Memoirs of Field-Marshal Lord Carver* (London: Hutchinson, 1989)

Carver, Michael (Field Marshal Lord) "Peacekeeping in Cyprus" in John T.A. Koumoulides (ed.) *Cyprus in Transition, 1960-1985* (London: Trigraph, 1986)

Choisi, Jeanette. "The Turkish Cypriot Elite: Its Social Function and Legitimation" *The Cyprus Review*, Volume 5, Number 2

Clerides, Glafcos. *Cyprus. My Deposition*, 4 Volumes (Nicosia: Alithea Press)

Clogg, Richard. *A Concise History of Greece* (Cambridge: Cambridge University Press, 1992)

Cordier, Andrew & Max Harrelson (eds.), *Public Papers of the Secretary-Generals of the United Nations. Volume VI, U Thant, 1961-64* (New York: Columbia University Press, 1976)

Coufoudakis, Van. "United States Foreign Policy and the Cyprus Question; A case Study in Cold War Diplomacy", in Attalides (ed.) *Cyprus Reviewed* (Nicosia: The Jus Cypri Association, 1976)

Crawshaw, Nancy. *The Cyprus Revolt. An Account of the Struggle for Union with Greece* (London: George Allen & Unwin, 1978)

Crawshaw, Nancy. "Cyprus: The Political Background" in Koumoulides (ed.) *Cyprus in Transition 1960-1985* (London: Trigraph, 1986)

Denktash, Rauf R. *The Cyprus Triangle* (London: Allen & Unwin, 1988)

Deringil, Selim. "Turkish Foreign Policy since Ataturk" in Dodd, (ed.), *Turkish Foreign Policy. New Prospects* (Huntingdon: Eothen, 1992)

Dodd, Clement. *Cyprus. The Need for New Perspectives* (Huntingdon: Eothen, 1999)

Dodd, Clement (ed.) The Political Social and Economic Development of Northern Cyprus (Huntingdon: Eothen, 1993)

Dodd, Clement (ed.) *Turkish Foreign Policy. New Prospects* (Huntingdon: Eothen, 1992)

Durch, William J. (ed.) *The Evolution of UN Peacekeeping. Case Studies and Comparative Analysis* (London: Macmillan, 1993)

Eden, Anthony. *Full Circle* (London: Cassel & Company, 1960)

Ehrlich, Thomas. *Cyprus, 1958-1967* (London: OUP, 1974)

Fabian, Larry L. *Soldiers without Enemies. Preparing the United Nations for Peacekeeping* (Washington, DC: The Brookings Institution, 1971)

Faustmann, Hubert "The Historical Background to the UN's Involvement in Cyprus" in Oliver P. Richmond and James Ker-Lindsay (eds.) *The Work of the UN in Cyprus. Promoting Peace and Development* (Basingstoke: Palgrave Macmillan, 2001)

Foley, Charles. *Legacy of Strife. Cyprus from Rebellion to Civil War* (London: Penguin, 1964)

Foreign Affairs Select Committee of the House of Commons, Third Report, *Cyprus*, Session 1986-1987 (London: Her Majesty's Stationery Office, 1987)

Gromyko, A.A. *Only for Peace* (Oxford: Pergamon Press, 1979)

Harbottle, Michael. The Impartial Soldier; (Oxford University Press, 1970)

Hatzivassiliou, Evanthis. "Blocking Enosis: Britain and the Cyprus Question, March-December 1956" *The Journal of Imperial and Commonwealth History*, Volume XIX, Number 2, 1991

Heinze, Christian. *Cyprus Conflict, 1964-1985*. (London: K Rustem, 1986)

Higgins, Rosalyn. United Nations Peacekeeping 1946-67. Documents and Commentary. Volume I: The Middle East (London: Oxford University Press, 1969)

Higgins, Rosalyn. United Nations Peacekeeping. Documents and Commentary. Volume IV: Europe 1946-79 (Oxford: Oxford University Press, 1981)

Hill, Sir George. *A History of Cyprus*, 4 Volumes (Cambridge: CUP, 1952)

Hitchens, Christopher. *Hostage to History. Cyprus from the Ottomans to Kissinger* (New York: The Noonday Press, 1989)

Holland, Robert. "Never, Never Land: British Colonial Policy and the Roots of the Violence in Cyprus, 1950-54" *The Journal of Imperial and Commonwealth History*, Volume XXI, Number 3, September 1993

Holland, Robert. *Britain and the Revolt in Cyprus, 1954-59* (Oxford: OUP, 1998)

Hunt, Sir David (ed.) *Footprints in Cyprus. An Illustrated History* (London: Trigraph, 1990)

Hunt, Sir David. "Independence and Invasion, 1960-" in: Sir David Hunt (ed.) *Footprints in Cyprus. An Illustrated History* (London: Trigraph, 1990)

James, Alan. *Peacekeeping in International Politics* (London: Macmillan, 1990)

James, Alan. *The Politics of Peacekeeping* (New York: Frederick A. Praeger, 1969)

James, Alan. *Keeping the Peace in the Cyprus Crisis, 1963-64* (Basingstoke: Palgrave Macmillan, 2002)

Joseph, Joseph S. *Cyprus. Ethnic Conflict and International Concern* (Basingstoke: Macmillan, 1997).

Joseph, Joseph S. "The UN as an Instrument of National Policy: The Case of Cyprus" *The Cyprus Review*, Volume 1, Number 2, Fall 1989

Joseph, Joseph S. 'Makarios as an International Power Broker'; *Mediterranean Quarterly*, Volume 13, Number 1, Spring 1992.

Ker-Lindsay, James. *The Origins of the United Nations Force in Cyprus (UNFICYP)* (PhD Thesis, University of Kent at Canterbury, 1997)

Khrushchev, Nikita (trans. Strobe Talbott). *Khrushchev Remembers. The Last Testament* (Boston: Little, Brown and Company, 1974)

Kinross, Patrick. *Ataturk. Rebirth of a Nation* (London: Weidenfeld, 1993)

Koumoulides, John T.A. (ed.) *Cyprus in Transition 1960-1985* (London: Trigraph, 1986)

Kyrris, Costas P. *History of Cyprus* (Nicosia, Proodos, 1988)

Laipson, Ellen. "Cyprus: A Quarter Century of US Diplomacy" in John T. A. Koumoulides (ed.) *Cyprus in Transition 1960-1985* (London: Trigraph, 1986)

Lewis, Bernard. *The Emergence of Modern Turkey* (Oxford: OUP, 1961)

Luard, Evan. *A History of the United Nations, Volume 2. The Age of Decolonization, 1955-1965* (London: Macmillan, 1989)

Markides, Diana Weston. "Britain's 'New Look' Policy for Cyprus and the Makarios-Harding Talks, January 1955-March 1956" *The Journal of Imperial and Commonwealth History*, Volume 23, Number 3, September 1995

Markides, Diana Weston. *Cyprus 1957-63. From Colonial Conflict to Constitutional Crisis. The Role of the Municipal Issue*. Minnesota Mediterranean and East European Monographs, Number 8 (Minnesota: University of Minnesota, 2001)

Markides, Kyriacos C. *The Rise and Fall of the Cyprus Republic* (London: Yale University Press, 1977)

Mayes, Stanley. *Makarios* (London: [n.p.], 1981)

Michaelides, Michael. "The Turkish Cypriot Working Class and the Cyprus Labour Movement" *The Cyprus Review*, Volume 5, Number 2, 1994

Moran, Michael (ed.) *Rauf Denktash at the United Nations. Speeches on Cyprus* (Huntingdon: The Eothen Press, 1997),

Moran, Michael. *Sovereignty Divided. How the Turkish Cypriots were Deprived of their Constitutional Rights* (Lefkosa: CYREP, December 1995)

Necatigil, Zaim M. *The Cyprus Question and the Turkish Position in International Law* (Oxford: Oxford University Press, 1989)

Newman, Edward. *The UN Secretary-General from the Cold War to the New Era. A Global Peace and Security Mandate?* (Basingstoke: Macmillan, 1998)

Nicolet, Claude. *United States Policy towards Cyprus, 1954-1974. Removing the Greek-Turkish Bone of Contention*, Peleus 9 (Mannheim und Mohnesee: Bibliopolis, 2001)

Oberling, Pierre. *The Cyprus Tragedy* (London: [n.p.], 1989)

Packard, Martin. "Cyprus 1964: Subversion of a Mission" in Dimitris Bourantonis and Marios Evriviades (eds.) *A United Nations for the Twenty-First Century. Peace Security and Development* (London: Kluwer Law International, 1996)

Packard, Martin. "Cyprus: UN Success or UN failure? Lessons for the Future"; Paper presented at '*The United Nations. Peace, Security and Development beyond the Year 2000*', Delphi, May 18-20 1995.

Panteli, Stavros. *A New History of Cyprus* (London: East-West Publications, 1984)

Papadopoulos, Andrestinos N. *Peace-Making and Peace-Keeping by the United Nations. Cyprus. A Case Study* (Nicosia: [n.p.], 1969)

Parsons, Sir Anthony. *From Cold War to Hot Peace. UN Interventions 1947-1994* (London: M Joseph, 1995)

Polyviou, Polyvios G. *Cyprus. The Tragedy and the Challenge* (London: John Swain & Son Ltd., [n.d.])

Purcell, H.D. *Cyprus* (London: Ernest Benn Ltd., 1969)

Reddaway, John. *Burdened With Cyprus. The British Connection* (London: Weidenfeld & Nicolson, 1986)

Richmond, Oliver P. *Mediating in Cyprus. The Cypriot Communities and the United Nations* (London: Frank Cass, 1998)

Richmond, Oliver P. and James Ker-Lindsay (eds.) *The Work of the UN in Cyprus. Promoting Peace and Development* (Basingstoke: Palgrave Macmillan, 2001)

Rikhye, Indar Jit and Michael Harbottle and Bjorn Egge. *The Thin Blue Line. International Peacekeeping and its Future* (London: Yale University Press, 1974)

Salih, Halil Ibrahim. *Cyprus. The Impact of Diverse Nationalism on a State* (Alabama: University of Alabama Press, 1978)

Smith, Martin A. "At Arm's Length: NATO and the United Nations in the Cold War Era" *International Peacekeeping*, 2:1 (1995)

Sonyel, Salahi R. *Cyprus. The Destruction of a Republic. British Documents, 1960-65* (Huntingdon: The Eothen Press, 1997)

Sonyel, Salahi R. "New Light on the Genesis of the Conflict: British Documents, 1960-67" in Clement H. Dodd (ed.) *Cyprus. The Need for New Perspectives* (Huntingdon: The Eothen Press, 1999), pp.21-22

Stegenga, James. *The United Nations Force in Cyprus* (Ohio: Ohio State University Press, 1968)

Stephens, Robert. *Cyprus. A Place of Arms* (London: Pall Mall Press, 1966)

Tamkoc, Metin. *The Turkish Cypriot State. The Embodiment of the Right to Self-Determination* (London: K Rustem and Brother, 1988)

Tornaritis, Criton G. *Cyprus. Its Constitutional and Other Legal Problems*, 2nd Edition (Nicosia: [n.p.], 1980)

U Thant. *View From the UN* (London:[n.p.], 1976)

Urquhart, Brian. *A Life in Peace and War* (London: Weidenfeld and Nicolson, 1987)

Urquhart, Brian. *Ralph Bunche. An American Life* (New York: WW Norton, 1993)

Vanezis, Procopios N. *Cyprus. The Unfinished Agony* (London: Abelard-Schuman, 1977)

Vanezis, Procopios N. *Makarios Life and Leadership* (London: Abelard-Schuman, 1979)

Verrier, Anthony. "Cyprus: Britain's Security Role", *The World Today*, March 1964

Verrier, Anthony. *International Peacekeeping. United Nations Forces in a Troubled World* (London: Penguin Books, 1981)

Vlachos, Angelos. *Deka Chronia Kypriakou* [Ten Years of the Cyprus Problem] (Athens: Estia Publishing, 1980)

Wainhouse, David W. *International Peace Observation. A History and Forecast* (Baltimore: Johns Hopkins Press, 1966)

White, N.D. *Keeping the Peace. The United Nations and the Maintenance of International Peace and Security* (Manchester: Manchester University Press, 1993)

Windsor, Phillip. *NATO and the Cyprus Crisis*, Adelphi Paper No. 14 (London: Brasseys' for the International Institute for Strategic Studies, 1964)

Woodhouse, C.M. *Modern Greece. A Short History* (London: Faber and Faber, 1991)

Xydis, Stephen G. *Cyprus. Conflict and Reconciliation 1954-1958* (Columbus: Ohio State University Press, 1967)

Yavuz, M. Haken "The Evolution of Ethno-Nationalism in Cyprus under the Ottoman and British Systems" *The Cyprus Review*, Volume 3, Number 2, Fall 1991

Index